Being an Effective Academic

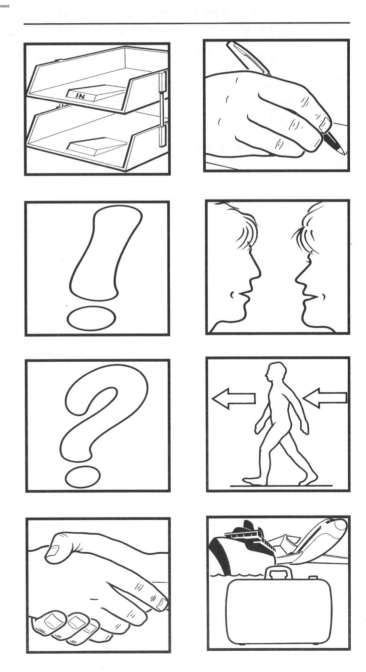

Leslie Johnson

© Oxford Centre for Staff Development 1996

Published by
THE OXFORD CENTRE FOR STAFF DEVELOPMENT
Oxford Brookes University
Gipsy Lane
Headington
Oxford
OX3 0BP

Being an Effective Academic
ISBN 1 873576 30 7
British Library Cataloguing-in-Publication Data. A catalogue record for this book is available from the British Library.

Designed and Typeset in 10 on 12.5pt Palatino and Helvetica by Ann Trew

Printed in Great Britain by
Oxonian Rewley Press Ltd
Oxford

Printed on paper produced from sustainable forests.

The Oxford Centre for Staff Development

Being an Effective Academic

Leslie Johnson

Contents

Contents

About the author

Leslie Johnson is Professor of Information Management at Brunel University. At the time of publication he is on study leave pursuing funded research. He was Dean of the Faculty of Science and Head of the Department of Computer Science at Brunel University. In September 1994 became Director of the Canterbury Business School, University of Kent at Canterbury.

As a young man he worked in industry and gained business qualifications. His first degree was in philosophy and his doctorate was in the theory of knowledge. He has published widely in computer science, cybernetics and information management. He is best known for his work on knowledge-based systems. His teaching duties over the years have ranged from courses on the philosophy of mind for the Department of Psychology to mathematical logic for the School of Mathematics. Most of his teaching and research have been directed towards understanding the nature of practical reasoning and enhancing its effectiveness.

Professor Johnson has been involved with the Enterprise in Higher Education Initiative at Brunel and has acquired an abiding interest in the aims and methods of higher education as a practical and theoretical pursuit.

Acknowledgements

The great great-grandfather of the ideas in this book was Benjamin Franklin. Reading his autobiography and some of his works started me on the road that led to writing this. The various great-grandfathers and fathers of this area are well-known figures too: William James (on habits), Peter Drucker (on management), Dale Carnegie (on just about everything). Most books of this kind owe something, either directly or indirectly, to these figures.

This is not a work of scholarship but I am aware of some of the fairly direct influences on my thinking: Steven Covey's Seven Habits of Highly Effective People (Simon and Schuster 1989) and Principled-Centred Leadership (Simon and Schuster 1990); Donald Clifton and Paula Nelson's Play to your Strengths (BCA 1992); J.Edward and Paul Schoemaker's Confident Decision Making (Guild Publishing 1989); and Roger Fisher and William Ury's Getting to YES (Business Books 1986).

Graham Gibbs helped bring this book to publication and made useful comments on the text. Mr Tremaine Cornish read an early draft and corrected several errors.

None of the people mentioned here is responsible for how I have made their ideas mine and the way I have chosen to convey them.

Introduction

There are organised and effective people of every personality type, just as there are successful managers of every personality type. So this book is for you.

The subject matter of this book

If you want to improve your effectiveness, I can guarantee that this book will offer ways of doing it that interest you. However, you will not find here any tricks or magic formulas, because the subject of the book is really you and your work, and most of the sections will not be complete until you make them your own.

To get the most of out the book

Many of the sections suggest things that are easy to do and have proven their worth, but even the simplest idea cannot work for you unless you want it to.

- Read each section actively (see § 5.5 Reading articles). Ask yourself how you could apply the idea.

- Make notes in the book, scribble and draw and make the material yours. When you decide to try something, be specific: write 'Immediately, I will schedule important but not pressing events in my timetable.' 'At the next opportunity I will listen actively,' and so on.

- Think about how you can make attractive to yourself the first steps of something new.

- If you try something that appeals to you, reward yourself and celebrate your successes.

- Schedule review periods and return to the book every month (see § 5.8 Review periods).

- Use the book as a handbook to help you when you are thinking about what to do or when you have a problem.

- If you drive to work, consider reading through your book item by item noting your writings and drawings and talk to yourself on a tape. Say what you think and tell yourself what you have resolved to do. Play the tape in your car on the way to work.

The most important thing, however, is to read with a pen in your hand and use it.

1   Basic self organisation

Being organised does not mean being tidy, does not mean paying attention to detail, does not mean constricting yourself and stifling your creativity, and it does not mean that you are a certain type of person. Being organised is not about diaries, filing cabinets and so on, it is about you and your work. It is about you being effective in your work.

It is easy to start to be better organised. When you see the benefits you will be motivated to continue. Being organised is a skill. Like all skills, being organised is not simply a matter of finding things out, it is a matter of application and practice. As you develop your system you become more effective and less stressed.

Right now, however, the important thing is your first step and not the nebulous horizon. Start now.

3

1.1 Dealing with paper

We spend a great deal of our time dealing with paper. Dealing with paper effectively is considered by many as an essential element in being more effective overall. It is certainly an unavoidable part of being an academic. Paying attention to it will be repaid greatly.

An easy start

Make an easy start to dominating your paperwork: take all your papers scattered around and put them into four piles:

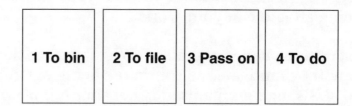

| 1 To bin | 2 To file | 3 Pass on | 4 To do |

To bin

Things to discard are copies of anything you intend to deal with 'some-day'. If you can live with the consequences of discarding it, discard it. Consider adopting the policy of not filing for yourself anything which someone else files as part of their duties.

To file

You will find it easier to file when your files are well organised and have recently been cleared of all surplus material.

Pass on

If you think that the paperwork is better dealt with or filed elsewhere, pass it on. Attach a slip making clear what the recipient should do and the reason why you are passing it on. If you think the recipient will be surprised that you are passing it on, arrange to meet them and get their views on the best way to deal with the item. Take the relevant paper work with you.

To do

To deal with this pile, you need to create action files which you keep close to hand. Mark these files: 'To Read', 'Correspondence', 'Meetings', 'Projects'. (Consider creating a 'Brought Forward' action file (see § 1.3 'Brought Forward' file).)

As you work through the To Do pile you will create a To Do list and place items in your action files. Your To Do list is very important as it helps you to deal with things in order of priority and frees you from the very real stress and inefficiency induced through having to remember what to do.

Take each item in turn:

• decide how you should deal with it,

• write a reminder on a To Do list,

• place the item in the appropriate action file.

Do not deal with it yet.

4

Priorities

When you have a clear desk you should look at what there is to do. Planning what to do ensures that you are effective. You should plan to do what you evaluate as offering the greatest payoff:

- Go through your To Do list and mark each item A, B or C. The A's should be pressing and important things to do. The B's should be the things that are important but are not so pressing. The C's and all the other things.

- Review your list daily; select the item with the highest payoff. (See § 2.4 Your 'To Do' list.)

Your in-tray

You will have guessed that, after this start, all incoming mail is dealt with in a similar way.

It has been shown that papers in an in-tray on your desk are distracting. If possible, put, and keep, your in-try behind you. The in-tray is the place where you keep all paperwork until you are ready to decide how to deal with it. Do not use the in-tray as an action file.

When you are ready, take each item in turn and decide whether to:

- bin it,

- file it,

- pass it on,

- place it in an action file and put a reminder in your To Do list.

For items that are placed in your action files, decide on the order of priority.

In this way you will handle most items once. Those that will be handled again will be associated with your To Do list and will be dealt with according to your priorities.

A clear desk

It is by dealing with paper in this way that you can keep a clear desk. No matter how important your paperwork is, you can only concentrate on one thing at a time. Having all your paperwork on your desk cannot help you do that. If you have processed your papers you know that everything is recorded in your To Do list and is to hand (but not to eye).

If you refrain from using your desk as an action file, you are relieved of distraction and the stress of worrying about forgetting what to do.

1.2 Constructing a classification system

In order to deal effectively with paper, you need to design a classification system for filing and make a routine that works for you. The first thing to do is to think about your work and construct a classification system for your activities. Doing this benefits you in more ways than one.

In one sense, thinking about what your work is, specifically, is the actual foundation of being effective. Thus, although it is relatively easy to construct a classification system it does need explicit thought and a little care.

How to establish your main classification headings

1 Identify the overall requirements of your job. What are the main areas where you have to perform professionally?

2 Go through your To Do list and try to come up with groupings that make sense.

3 Ask yourself the following questions:

   • What activities bring recognition?

   • What are my responsibilities and level of authority?

   • Where can I contribute by getting results that are valued by my department and myself?

You should, by this process, cover all the aspects of your job. Consider supplementing the list by personal things like 'home, family and friends', 'hobbies' and 'personal profile'. Organise the areas under about seven headings, including your personal headings. (It has been established that fewer than ten top-level headings are optimum.) These are your main headings. All your activities can now be grouped and placed under one of a smallish number of main headings. Some of these headings are likely to be ones not related to any specific post or function you have, but general to any academic. Others should be more specific to your post or function. You should not include things which are beyond your sphere of responsibility or level of authority. Your task is to become personally well organised and for this you should conceive as your main areas all (but only) those things you do for which you have a professional commitment and delegated responsibility.

What are your responsibilities as a professional? What are your delegated responsibilities and levels of authority? These questions may not be simple to answer, and you may have to involve a mentor, your Head of Department or Dean.

At your appraisal interview you can share your concept of your main areas of activity, and obtain feedback and agree basic objectives.

A list of categories to get you started

Although it is no substitute for your going through the above process, the following list may help you to get started. Any of these headings or subheadings may be eliminated, or combined with another.

Administration	senior tutor work placements admissions procedures timetabling examinations conveyor	course director publicity library representative research convenor interviewing
Teaching	teaching portfolio evaluations and review	reading lists tutoring

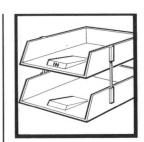

Research	projects X, Y, Z references and notes	supervision proposals
Personal and professional development	foreign languages teaching methods research methods life skills health and fitness professional up-dating	new technology assessment methods general scholarship rest and relaxation good citizenship personal organisation
Budget	monitoring purchasing	resource allocation annual budget
Staff	individuals X,Y, Z appraisal	recruitment teaching duties
Large one-offs	introducing information technology introducing a new course introducing organisational change organising relocation or refurbishing ideas	
Internal relations	committee memberships co-operation with HoD and peers co-operation with other departments co-operation with central administration	
External relations	committee memberships co-operation with outside organisations assistance or service honorary positions consultancies editorships/panels	
Planning	annual review and planning long-term planning and strategy changes in organisational and financial structure staff participation adaptation to trends transition to new technology student numbers and staff levels financial forecasting staff development activities space requirements	

Remember, any of these headings or subheadings may be eliminated, or combined with another. For example, new lecturers will not have Budget, Staff and Planning as main headings, but may have a 'talk-to' list as part of Internal relations, and 'adaptation to trends' as part of Professional development. You might decide that Internal and External relations can be combined into Communications but that an outside appointment needs a separate main heading. You might find that none of the administrative functions are right for you; even the HoD may find this, if all the main functions have been delegated to members of staff (on the other hand HoDs are certain to have Staff and Planning main headings). In this case an HoD might put general administration under Internal Relations.

7

1.3 'Brought Forward' file

You often need some sort of reminder of what to do on a particular day, or you need papers for a meeting sometime in the future, and so on. A Brought Forward file is a delivery system for these types of item.

The file itself

You need a concertina file with pockets numbered 1 through to 31. They can be purchased from most large stationers.

How to use a Brought Forward file

You use a Brought Forward file to post to yourself items for delivery at a specified date.

Say you want to remind yourself that a student promised an essay on 5 March:

- write a note to yourself as a reminder;
- write 'March' on the top corner of the note;
- put it into the pocket numbered 5, for the fifth.

Say you want a set of papers for a meeting on 3 April:

- write 'April' on the top corner of the papers;
- put them in the pocket numbered 3.

Say there is an article you intend to read while you are travelling to a meeting on 7 June:

- write 'June' on the top corner;
- put it into the pocket numbered 7.

Each day you look into the file and those items for that date are there for you – the month is written on the relevant pieces. There might be other items for other months, but that doesn't matter. They will still be there when you need them.

If you have many items to take forward

If you have many items to carry forward, consider obtaining two concertina files: one for the months of the year and one for the days of the month. You place each item in the pocket for the appropriate month. At the beginning of each month, you empty that month's pocket and place each item in the appropriately numbered pocket of the other file.

1.4 Filing

The purpose of storage is retrieval. Your filing system should have a structure that reflects your work and makes it easy to file and retrieve items.

Classification

Every item should fall under one of the major headings which reflect your needs and responsibilities. Do not have too many sub-divisions under any major heading as it increases the chance that an item will be misfiled. Review your system (see § 1.2 Constructing a classification system).

Starting out

When you have decided on your system, you will need to physically reorganise your files. It is best to empty your files, thin them out, and refile the material to fit your system. Anything you file should be marked with a discard date. Deciding the discard date as you do the filing encourages you not to hoard and makes thinning out easier. You should thin out your files at least once a year. Schedule an afternoon. Perhaps you can persuade the whole department to do this on the same day and arrange for the paper to be taken away for recycling.

Action files

To deal with the in-tray, you need action files which you keep close at hand:

- in your desk,
- in your desk hanging files, or
- in folders in trays behind you.

Mark these files:

- 'To Read',
- 'Correspondence',
- 'Meetings',
- 'Projects',
- 'To File'.

(For a large project you should have a separate action file in addition to the other files in your filing system; the other files should only be used for reference material and completed work.)

A 'By Date' file

There is some evidence that we remember things well by approximate date. Consider classifying memos or other types of correspondence by the month sent or received. You could use a concertina file with pockets marked by the months. The advantage of this By Date file is that you can use it for a year and then archive it whole and start a new one.

Routine filing

Get into the habit of putting an archive date or discard date on your documents. Do not let your To File file overflow. File a few items between appointments and at other odd moments. Always clear the filing at the end of the week.

1.5 Desk organisation

Diary

The fundamental time periods in an academic's life seem to be the hour, the week, the term or semester, and the academic year. Most cycles of activities have these periods. There are academic diaries and organisers which open out to two pages per week; these are very convenient and perhaps the best for most academics.

Address book

You may find it is easier to sort addresses and telephone numbers alphabetically within a category rather than in a single alphabetical sequence. Consider the following areas:

Clubs and Societies	Hotels and restaurants
Colleagues	Professional
Contacts	Projects X, Y, Z
Emergency	Suppliers
Family	Transport
Friends	Tutees

You can use continuous white correction tape to change an entry without rewriting the whole sheet. If you have a computer you can maintain your address list there and print it from time to time.

Desk file

Keep a desk file containing today's schedule, today's To Do reminders and today's papers sorted.

Notes

Keep a note pad with you at all times and use it when things occur to you; transcribe or transfer items to your lists when you are at your desk.

Stationery

All paper, including lists, notepads, etc., and pens should be placed in a drawer or, if you prefer a 'desk tidy' and desk file. An organiser, however, will do duty for all of these.

Organiser

An organiser is a tool and a system of dealing with things that you can adapt to your purposes. The organiser consists of a ring binder and:

- various diaries,

- an address book, and

- a box of forms which can be added or removed from the organiser.

An organiser encourages you to deal with things in a way which integrates your plans, fixed schedules, information, diary and address book resources. Your system exploits these and other resources in order to help you decide on, and to pursue, your goals.

To get you started

To begin with, an organiser is very unfamiliar and can seem to demand too much discipline to keep up. Organisers do, in fact, demand a certain minimum discipline but they are used with great effect by all sorts of people, from artists to sports champions, professionals to students. The easy way to get started is to keep it simple:

- Transfer your existing system into an organiser.

- Timetable periods when you will develop and refine your system over, say, a year. Consider starting each month with a new aspect and developing and refining that aspect.

You need not purchase an organiser, a loose-leaf ring binder with plastic wallets and dividers can be a very versatile and cheap organiser. Although it doesn't look like an organiser, it is one. An organiser is a tool which figures in a method of working; it need not be a specifically designed product and accessories.

1.6 Paper vs personal computer

It is not easy to decide whether to use software tools and how best to use them. First you should think clearly about the way you work. Then consider which of the things you do are candidates for computer support. The table below will help to start you off in the right way and at the right level of abstraction.

	Paper systems	PC systems
Information	Quick and easy to enter	Calling up the system and entering information takes time and can be inconvenient
	The information cannot be manipulated	The information can be sorted, cut and pasted, reformatted. It can be retrieved in different ways
	Easy to scan and review Often quick and easy to find	Information is not easy to scan and takes time to come up on the screen
Organising	Things need to be entered in more than one place or transferred from one place to another and need cross-referencing with the diary	Tasks are automatically scheduled. Changes can be propagated to all relevant places
	Methods of working can be changed quickly	Changing ways of working can mean a great deal of work in reconfiguring the system
	In project management, not easy to get an overview	Large projects can be given a better overview

After you have thought carefully about the way you work you should consider what packages, if any, you could use.

The basic software packages

Word-processing

Word-processors are so good now that there is no reason not to use one.

- Get a word-processor that is fast and easy to use. Don't buy a word-processor with lots of features unless you really need them. (If you do need sophisticated features one day, then use your simple word-processor as support software to a desk-top publishing system. This combination is better than the best word-processor.)

- Ensure that your word-processor can output ASCII files (don't buy it otherwise).

- Make sure it has a spell-checker.

Spreadsheets

The spreadsheet is a very versatile piece of software that can range in function from a list manipulator to a simple database. Spreadsheets are extremely useful for designing mark sheets which do the various calculations automatically.

Database

The database package is the item of software most under-used by academics. Perhaps it is thought that databases are complicated to learn how to use and their use is justified only when manipulating large amounts of data. Neither of these ideas are true. Simple database packages are very easy to learn and are very powerful. They have a surprising versatility in useful, simple applications, like making a book catalogue, a contacts list, recording your publications data, maintaining your student lists and so on. Don't be afraid to make very simple uses of them.

Graphics

Drawing tools are now very sophisticated and enable you to make polished overheads. Some specialist packages are specially tailored to create presentation materials. A good graphics package is necessary support software to a desk-top publishing system.

Communications

Communications software is not only electronic mail; there are packages which link you into hundreds of databases and bulletin boards. In general, you pay for the telephone connect time and an additional time-linked charge.

Personal organisers

Automated organisers usually have a diary, address book, To Do list, a simple 'free text retrieval' database and a few toys. They are very hard to use successfully as your only organiser, but they have some very enthusiastic promoters.

Bundles

There are various 'office' or 'works' bundles of the basic packages. Each package in the bundle has the same 'look and feel' as the others and they can exchange data with one another relatively freely. Bundles are often extremely good value for money and comprehensive. They are suitable for most non-specialist needs and are your best first buy, even if you don't intend to use all of the packages, at first.

Exploiting the computer

Many computer users fail to exploit their computer's powers. They learn how to do the basics and stop there. The quick ways of doing interesting things need a little extra investment of time. With computers you cannot learn from experience. You need either to be shown or to learn how to read manuals. It is best to schedule time for getting to know the packages and their manuals.

13

2 Priorities

The priority you place on something is not a natural property you recognise in it. The priority you place on it is an expression of how doing it furthers your goals. The better you prioritise the more likely you are to realise your goals. By the same token, the better you know your goals the better you are able to prioritise.

An essential part of being effective is to devote your time in proportion to your priorities. The most difficult part of managing your time is linking your schedules and your To Do list to your priorities. This chapter helps you to set your priorities and to schedule your time accordingly.

15

2.1 What do you want?

The better you know your goals the better you are able to prioritise and the better you prioritise the more likely you are to achieve your goals. You need to be clear about what you want.

Your long-term goal *Sucssful acadmic, practitoner and a PhD*

Set the right goals. What do you want? How can you change yourself or your job so that you do more of what you want? Picture yourself as having achieved your goal. Make what you want concrete by actively visualising yourself having achieved what you want. Picture the sort of person will you be.

- What is your manner?

- What skills do you have?

- How do you dress?

- What strengths do you have?

- Do you have any of these traits now?

See yourself doing things that are possible for you. Goals should be such that they enhance your self-esteem and create a positive identity.

- Work at your vision of the future.

- What approach should you take and what would you have to do, or what do you have to be like, to achieve this?

- Break down your long-term goal into medium-term goals.

- Write it all down.

Through action and living, your long-term goal may change. You need to steer a course between having no goals at all and hanging on to goals that are no longer appropriate.

Medium-term goals

Think about medium-term goals in the context of your classification system (see § 1.2 Constructing a classification system).

- Are your headings right for your medium-term goals?

- Are your medium-terms goals right?

You might have to circle round your long-term and medium-term goals until you are satisfied that there is an approach to your goals that you can take.

Make your efforts manageable

Medium-term goals need time and effort to achieve them. Break down your medium-term goals into shorter-term ones.

Mastering basic information technology could be one of your sub-goals. The best strategy is to have a modest target of becoming familiar with the rudiments first and decide later what to pursue a little more deeply. Suppose your first priority is word- processing. Why not take an introductory course? How will you prepare for it? You may decide that after the course you will spend two hours a week on learning more about your word-processor and trying out some other packages (see § 2.3 What should you be doing this week?).

So, although learning about information technology needs time and effort and seems too large a task to undertake right now – you say to yourself that next year you'll have more time setting a modest target and taking a one day course on word-processing doesn't seem such a big task. Looking up something in the manual and spending a little time on useful play isn't too big a task either.

16

The edge effect

An attractive vision of future benefits cannot distract us from the first moment of change. The 'edge effect' is precisely the dominant focus of the mind on the near edge of change. To overcome the inhibiting effects of this:

- Make your first steps towards any goal as attractive and as easy as possible.

- Plan to give yourself a reward for having taken the first step.

Summary

- To achieve what you want, picture yourself after you have succeeded.

- Make your images concrete, specific, real. What would you have to do to be like this?

- Break down your goals into scheduled activities with specific performance criteria: prioritise and set yourself deadlines with specific achievements to be made.

- Make the first steps attractive and easy.

2.2 The areas of neglect

Which are the important activities?

Think of the important things which you do. If you have decided on your goals, you will find among the important things tasks associated with your long-term goals Other important activities are: exercise; rest and relaxation; building relationships; identifying new opportunities; preparation; thinking about and writing up your personal mission, your strengths, your weaknesses. All of these things are important but are not usually pressing, and it is easy to neglect them in the whirl of day-to-day activities.

Types of activities classified in a quadrant

	Pressing	Not pressing
Important	1 • Scheduled/deadline events, (e.g. teaching and examining) • Emergencies • References and refereeing • Seeing students • Reading reports and essays	2 • Building relationships • Self-organisation • Exercise • Rest and relaxation • Identifying new opportunities • Preparation • Research and publication • Medium-term goals
Not important	3 • Some meetings • Some mail • Some interruptions • Some requests and invitations	4 • Some phone calls • Some mail • Keeping busy (e.g. spending fruitless hours at a computer terminal) • Moaning and fussing • Pedantry • Subversive pleasures

The 'neglect' quadrant

The areas of neglect usually reside in the second quadrant the important, but not pressing, category. To make sure you do not neglect them, it is necessary for you to identify them. You need to be clear and explicit about what your work is, what you want to achieve and the values you and others cherish. You will probably need to cultivate certain professional attitudes and values too.

Map the things that you do, or should do, into quadrants

Think about what you actually do, or should do, and place the activities into the quadrants above. What you place where depends on your conception of what it is to be an academic, where you are working, and what your values are.

There are those without a sense of what it is to be a professional who, in a drive for personal efficiency, relegate important things like seeing students, to the pressing but not important quadrant. In this way time management can be used to subvert professional performance.

Undertake an audit

Ask yourself 'What important things am I neglecting?' Much of this book is an aid to helping you answer this question. The book also shows you some ways of stopping that neglect.

2.3 What should you be doing this week?

It is much easier to carry out individual projects, such as learning a language, when your learning activities are scheduled. You don't have to think about doing them, you just follow your schedule. Your timetable should reflect what you have put in your second quadrant of activities (important but not immediately pressing, see § 2.2).

You must add your own events to your calendar and weekly timetable as fixed by others. A week's timetable for an active research member of staff might then look like the following.

Timetable: First semester

Monday

8.45	Review and day planning
9.00 -10.00	Lesson in Word-processing, etc.
10.00	
12.00	Deal with mail
12.30	Practice WP
12.50	Lunch and a walk
1.30	Phone calls/short meetings
2.00	Lecture on CS 490
3.00	Seminar with Group A
5.00	Meeting with research group

Late evening: swimming

Tuesday

8.45	Review and day planning
9.15	Large tasks when not at Senate meeting
12.30	Lunch appointments
2.00	PhD supervision: HN
3.00	
5.00	Meeting with students
9.00 -11.00	Preparing teaching material

Wednesday

8.45	Review and day planning
9.00	Research
12.30	Practise WP
12.50	Lunch and a walk
1.30	Phone calls/short meetings
2.00	Planning (or departmental meeting monthly)
3.30	
5.30	Swimming with kids
7.30	Dinner out or take-away at home

Thursday

8.45	Review and day planning
9.00	Private study
10.00	PhD supervision: HH
12.30	Practise WP
12.50	Lunch and a walk
1.30	Phone calls/short meetings
2.00	
3.00	Lecture CS 490
4.00	At home for students
5.00	Reading/looking for new ideas
9.00 -11.00	Preparing teaching material

Friday

8.45	Review and day planning
9.00	Research
10.00	Ph.D supervision: REJ
11.00	Research
12.30	Practise WP
12.50	Lunch and a walk
1.30	Phone calls/short meetings
2.00	Research
5.00	Filing and review next week's timetable

Late evening: swimming

Saturday

Morning: shopping/walk

Late afternoon: writing

Evening: watch a TV film with kids

Sunday

Late afternoon: writing

Notes (reminders)
- Practise juggling in spare moments each day
- Do a little filing at odd moments

Notes (locations)
- CS 490 is in Lecture Centre 067
- Seminar is in M116
- Research meeting in my office
- Departmental meetings in M217

19

This person's timetable caters for all the important but not pressing areas of their work, leaving time to select and execute items on their To Do list and cater for the unexpected. No time is wasted waiting for the muse or wondering what to do; the person follows their timetable like a good professional writer who writes '1500 words at day, starting at nine', confident that they could not be using their time better.

There are parts of the year when you will not be teaching. Do a timetable for these weeks as well. You may want to save some big jobs for these weeks and block out days and half-days, but you should still make sure that your timetable meets all your needs. Don't neglect other things that are important.

In timetabled periods, put off being interrupted and say to callers 'I'm busy right now can I call you back at . . . ?' or 'could you come back at . . . .?' Not only does this help you keep to your priorities, but you let others know that you are aware of your time and this helps them to value it too.

20

2.4 Your 'To Do' list

Compile and maintain a list of all your projects, tasks and assignments. Put in due dates. This list in not an action plan, it is an aide-memoire. This is time efficient because you do not waste time thinking about what to do or find yourself reacting to events for which you are poorly prepared.

Part of a To Do list showing deadline, date completed and priority

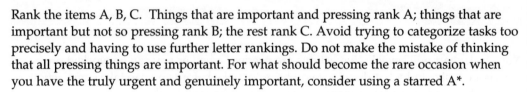

To Do:			
Write reference for A. N. Other	asap		B
	13 Oct		
Complete questionnaire on use of quality procedures	20 Oct		C
Phone Graham Gibbs about running a workshop	30 Oct		B
on how to be an organised academic			
Send page proofs back to printer	asap		A
	12 Oct		

Rank the items A, B, C. Things that are important and pressing rank A; things that are important but not so pressing rank B; the rest rank C. Avoid trying to categorize tasks too precisely and having to use further letter rankings. Do not make the mistake of thinking that all pressing things are important. For what should become the rare occasion when you have the truly urgent and genuinely important, consider using a starred A*.

Tick an item when you start work on it. Double tick and date it when you have finished.

Pareto's principle

A principle first propounded by Vilfredo Pareto is that 20% of what you do yields 80% of the results and conversely 80% of what you do yields only 20% of the results.

Pareto's principle is a useful notion to keep in mind when setting priorities. Give preference to high pay-off tasks which promise to yield substantial benefits. Neglecting these usually has no short-term consequences. That is why they are often neglected. It is important to note that some tasks have negative impact, if they are put off. For example, doing what needs doing to initiate projects with long lead times.

Your diary

Transfer items from your master list to your diary page or day planner, having due regard to the priorities and deadlines. Schedule the most important items for the time of day you are at your best for that kind of item. Do not try to pack in too many items. Leave yourself time to accommodate the unexpected tutee with a genuine problem or a really welcome telephone call, and so on. You can always fill in gaps with small items.

21

2.5 Larger tasks or assignments

The To Do list idea can be extended to cover your larger tasks and assignments.

Task charts

1 Take, or modify, a blank To Do list and make a task statement across the top.

2 Identify the objective and write it out in the first section.

3 Break the task down into parts. Sometimes it helps to think backwards from the goal to initial steps. Arrange the steps in a logical order and enter them on the task sheet; steps may be sub-tasks which require their own task chart.

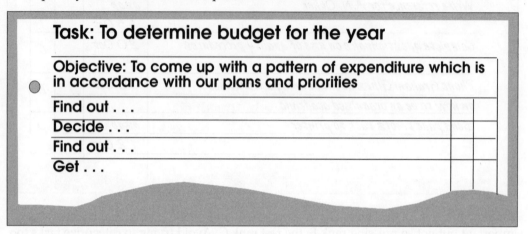

Your task chart will reveal what actions are needed, whether any can be worked on simultaneously, and what decisions you have to make before you can take some action. Your task chart is a useful resource which you can share with others.

4 Schedule time in your timetable.

5 Transfer to your diary those items that should be in hand before the task can be started.

Action planning

Whenever possible treat your goals and larger tasks as needing action planning (see Chapter 4). Identify targets and use explicit success criteria.

22

3 Decision making

Decisive decision making demands a type of judgement that needs practice and can be improved.

The first two and the final sections of this chapter deal with the decision-making process. The remaining sections describe and recommend the use of various aids to the decision-making process. Some of these aids consolidate the individual choices of a group, others encourage discussion and agreement. Section 3.4, on deciding group priorities, gives a form of decision making that combines both of these approaches.

Even a modest attempt to master some of the ideas in this chapter will enable you to make better decisions, more easily and with less stress, and to contribute to group decision-making processes more effectively.

3.1 The decision-making process

Decision making is an activity which might be undertaken by you as an individual or by you as part of a group. In either case it is now understood that the quality of decision making is improved by simply being more explicit about the decision-making process and giving some consideration to each part of it.

First, it is useful to know about the types of decision-making errors that occur frequently.

Typical decision making errors

- Jumping in without even a few moments' thought about what the real issue is and how the decision should be made.

- Failing to define the problem in more ways than one.

- Failing to seek key information because you are too sure of your assumptions and opinions.

- Relying too much on convenient facts.

- Failing to follow a systematic procedure.

- Failing to record and evaluate evidence and hence learn from the past. People overestimate the degree to which they control events, and when things go well think it is the result of their efforts. On the other hand, if things go badly they create an explanation of the result which takes it beyond their control. These biases make learning from experience difficult.

To avoid these errors you need to review how you take decisions. The key effective decision-making processes are as follows. Even cursory attention to these will improve your decision making and make it more likely that your decisions will be good.

The vital first step

When faced with a decision, the first thing you should do is explicitly consider the decision-making process itself and make choices about it.

Ask yourself:

- What is the real or primary issue?

- To deal with this, what is the most important aspect of the decision-making process (the mental set I have, finding the facts, drawing conclusions, getting feedback)?

- In general, how should decisions like this be made?

- Does this decision have wide, perhaps hidden, impact?

- Does it have to be made now? By me?

- Are there examples of similar or related decisions that I can learn from?

- Do I have personal needs, limitations or biases which might distort the decision-making process?

The three phases of coming to a conclusion

The decision-making process can be broken down into three parts. These need not be followed sequentially. You might move backwards and forwards over them as things become clearer.

1 Simplify the problem. You cannot avoid doing this. The mental set you have is a mechanism for simplifying a problem. Good decision makers are aware of this and explicitly think about the mental set from which they will look at the issue.

Ask yourself:

- What aspects of the situation do I leave out by the way I look at the issue?

- What success criteria do I really use?

- What metaphors am I using and what do they make me focus on?

- What other metaphors could be used?

- Why do I think about the issue this way?

- How do others think about the issue?

2   Get the information you require. Good decision makers realise that the information-gathering process is just as open to distortion as any other aspect of the decision-making process and guard against this. Most of us have an inclination to favour data that support our current beliefs and to dismiss evidence that overturns them.

Ask yourself:

- What evidence might change my opinions?

- How likely is it that my knowledge on the issue will be appropriate in the future?

- Why should I take greater confidence to be greater accuracy?

- Why should the available data be thought to be the best data?

- Why should I judge on the most recent evidence; what has been happening over the longer term?

- Am I letting the most vivid or emotionally charged event determine how I look at the whole issue?

- What am I taking as a reference point which determines what I think possible?

3   Draw conclusions. Good decision makers know that they make more accurate judgements when they follow systematic rules.

- Make decisions on what you have come to judge as a simple issue intuitively or with simple decision aids.

- When making an important decision, construct a 'linear system' for the choice (see § 3.7 Linear systems of making a choice).

25

3.2 Turning experience into learning

Learning from experience is very difficult. Your chances are improved if you learn not only from the events of the past but the process of decision making that produced them.

Be explicit

Events seem inevitable with hindsight and this hampers the ability to learn from experience. Approach issues in a way that increases your chance of learning:

- Explicitly define your goals, explicitly define success and failure, specify to what extent you believe your own efforts can influence the result.

- After the event, ask others how much of the success or failure they think you should accept.

- Record your successes and failures.

- For repeated decisions see if you can set up a statistical test to determine the role of chance.

A learning analysis

To overcome deficiencies in feedback you need to schedule regular sessions with the objective of answering the questions

- 'What have I learned?'

- 'What should I be learning, from recent experiences?'

Look for missing feedback

Much potentially useful feedback is missing. For example, the data on how well students who leave higher education without a degree do. We should ask what happens to those we do not select, or pass and so on. Similarly, when looking at any problem you should ask what feedback is missing.

Don't ignore feedback

Keeping and analysing accepted papers, successful grant proposals, job applications and so on is very rare. It is feedback ignored. When something is right, failing to find out why it is right is feedback ignored. You cannot build on strength when you have no feedback on success.

Beware of self-fulfilling prophecies

Often you influence the outcome of your decisions in ways that make the quality of the decisions themselves inaccessible. For example, deciding that a particular course is typically full of poor students makes it hard to judge whether their results are a product of their qualities or of your attitudes. Choosing someone as a protégé means increasing the chances of their success and this means that the quality of the original decision is not readily accessible to feedback. Bosses may not realise that the reason why they find more errors in the work of someone they mistrust is because they examine the work more closely and remember the errors easily. You need to think of ways of minimising the effect.

Summary

Good decision makers establish systems for learning from the past. They:

- record what they expect to happen;
- collect data on what happens;
- guard against self-serving explanations.

In short, good decision makers develop methods for converting experience into learning.

3.3 Check sheets

Many meetings spend too much time discussing matters of opinion when they should more properly be discussing matters of fact. It is very often a positive first step to stop speculation and agree on what data is relevant. Check sheets help you to do this.

The purpose of check sheets

Check sheets are a simple but powerful tool. You can use them:

- to develop a picture of the causes of a problem;

- to help you to arrive at a problem statement;

- as an aid to decision making.

They enable you to transform opinions into precise factual statements.

You can design a wide variety of check sheets: errors in proofs, interruptions per day for a week by type, participation in a seminar by person and type of participation, late draft examination papers by person over two semesters.

A simple example of a check sheet to record the results of teaching observation

Event	Lectures 3 to 6				Total
Smiled	IIIII IIIII II	IIIII	IIIII	IIIII IIII	31
Paused	IIIII IIII	IIIII I	IIIII IIII	II	26
Encouraged	IIII	II	III	I	10
Interrupted	IIIII IIIII	IIIII II	IIIII IIII	IIIII III	34
Opened up	I	II	III	I	7
Blocked visual	IIIII II	IIIII IIIII	IIIII IIIII I	IIIII II	35
Didn't listen	IIIII IIIII IIII	IIIII IIIII III	IIIII IIIII III	IIIII IIIII IIII	54

Designing a check sheet

If you were designing the check sheet shown above, the observer and the observe would have to:

1   Agree what events are to be checked.

2   Establish a time period over which the observations will be made.

3   Design a layout to suit your purpose.

Using a check sheet

Collect the data consistently and honestly; a group might have to look at examples in order to agree on what counts as what.

3.4 Deciding group priorities

You may be a member of a group that has undertaken an audit and identified a number of possible things for improvements but finds more than it can cope with in a single year. The group must decide which things to tackle first.

It often happens that the one who is most senior or shouts loudest determines what is worked on and a group does not feel committed. The following tool provides a technique which not only builds consensus but also helps the group to clarify the actual choices and the reasons in support of their selection.

1 If some problems have already been identified, write them up and ask the group to consider the list and add any other things they think important. You can do this in writing and ask for written responses, or have a meeting and use a flip-chart.

2 Put a letter before each problem statement. Ask each person to make a list with letters down one side.

3 Ask each member of the group to rank the options. If the number of options is greater than nine, consider asking them to rank only the first (n/2 + 1) options, placing all the others as 'equal last'. The first candidate is given the highest score.

4 Make a table from the individual lists and add the numbers across. The one with the highest score is ranked first, and so on. A group of five, with nine problem statements might generate a table like the one below. With this group, problems C, F and J rank as top priority.

A table used to determine ranking of items

Item & total		Peter	Paul	Mary	Janet	John
A	19	6	4	3	2	4
B	5	1	1	1	1	1
C	21	5	3	6	4	3
D	15	4	2	1	3	5
E	7	1	1	2	1	2
F	20	2	6	5	6	1
G	5	1	1	1	1	1
H	5	1	1	1	1	1
I	10	1	1	1	1	6
J	20	3	5	4	5	3

5 Take the top few priorities in turn, and consider:

• How big a job will it be? You may need to limit the number of major tasks.

• Should the task be staged or its scope increased?

• Are there natural links with other priorities? If so, make the most of them.

Setting out the answers to these questions in the form of yet another table helps in reaching a decision. The table has the possible priorities down one side and the criteria across the top. Enter relevant information in the table's cells.

3.5 Pairwise comparisons

It sometimes happens that you are in a group or on your own and do not really know how to go about choosing from a set of options. This is usually because you are not sure what are the right criteria for choosing. A useful method in this case is to pair options and make comparisons. Do not reason thus: ' We preferred A to B and B to C so we must prefer A to C.' You are trying to come to grips with the criteria and breaking down the problem to make it tractable. By making pairwise comparison you can do this. The scoring mechanism is illustrated in the following table.

A simple pairwise comparison table

	A	B	C	D	E
A 3		✓		✓	✓
B 2				✓	✓
C 3		✓		✓	✓
D 1					✓
E 0					
blanks down	5	3	5	2	1
✓ across	3	2	3	1	0
Sum	8	6	8	3	1

Method

1 Make a table out of the choices.

2 Compare the first with the second. If you judge the first better than the second, tick the cell. In the example A is judged better than B, D and E.

3 Go to the next line and repeat the process, and so on.

4 Count the blanks down and write the sum in the appropriate box and column.

5 Count the ticks across and write the sum in the appropriate box and column. In the illustration, there are 3 ticks across for A and you find '3' in the appropriate box in column A.

6 For each choice, sum the number of blanks down and the number of ticks across.

7 The choice with the largest sum is ranked first, and so on. In the event of a tie, go back and compare the two again.

With a large number of items, choosing something by this process can be extremely tedious.

Pairwise comparison is a good starting position for many decision-making activities. If you have a large number to choose from and you don't know where to start, take a sample of seven or eight, pairwise compare, and note your reasoning. Take the best few and use the characteristics of these as criteria to filter the rest to make a short-list (see § 3.6 Making a short-list). Use the pairwise comparison or some other method to choose from the short-list.

29

3.6 Making a short-list

With a large number of options or candidates to decide from, it is best to construct a filter to make a short-list. This is illustrated by a filter constructed for applications to a post in a university.

The criteria

It was decided to rate each candidate on the following criteria:

(a) Basic educational qualifications (degrees and professional qualifications).

(b) Relevance of qualifications to the field.

(c) Research training (with a PhD, a candidate would be given full marks).

(d) Published output.

(e) Teaching experience/quality.

(f) Relevant industrial experience.

(g) Fit to perceived needs of the department.

(h) Special characteristics.

(i) Introducing a new strategic option.

(j) Risk factors.

The ratings

It was agreed to rate the candidates on these criteria on a scale of -1 to 3, except in the case of risk, where the rating would be -3 to 1. Two professors and one senior lecturer independently rated all the candidates on these criteria. After discussion, a few adjustments were made to individual ratings and a composite was taken.

The filter

It was agreed that a filter of 12 points would be appropriate and this determined a long-list of fourteen candidates.

Dealing with the short-list

The long-list was discussed and reduced to a short-list of eight – those with a score of 3 on the fit with departmental needs, introducing new strategic options, or special characteristics. These candidates were invited to the department and later interviewed. After the interviews the appointments board discussed the candidates, paying particular attention to the representations of the department, and then each member of the board ranked the candidates. A composite ranking determined who was appointed.

Justification of the decision

The appointee was a woman from overseas. A justification for a work permit was made to the Home Office by submitting, among other things, the details of the decision-making process and criteria. The Home Office issued a work permit.

Generalisation

This story illustrates the use of a filter. When faced with making a choice from a large number of options you can construct a filter and then examine the long-list by some other method. Look at the short-list qualitatively.

3.7 Linear systems of making a choice

You cannot consistently make good decisions through unorganised judgements alone. Your random inconsistency and your inability to evaluate large quantities of evidence are your biggest problems. You need to find a systematic way to evaluate the evidence for and against each possible choice and then pick the one that your system indicates is the best.

Subjective linear systems

'Linear' is the term for combining separate pieces of evidence by addition or subtraction. A linear system of making a choice adds the things for, and subtracts the things against, the various options. We will illustrate what is involved in setting up and using a linear system by reference to a familiar example, that of student admissions.

Setting up your system

1   Determine what factors you consider provide evidence for or against the various choices.
    In this case, it is considered that A-levels, type and quality of work experience, motivation and interest as shown in an interview and the support given in the references are the evidence which indicate whether an applicant is likely to complete the course successfully.

2   For each factor, devise a method of converting data into a percentage grade where 0 represents the lowest possible score and 100 represents the highest.
    In this case, a scheme for converting A-level grades into percentage points was devised, where three A-levels at grade A is 100 percentage points and anything less than two A-levels at grade E is 0. For the interview data, a standard form was designed on which the interviewer graded the motivation, interest and aptitude of the applicant with simple letter grades. A method of converting these grades into percentage points was agreed. And so on.

3   Determine the weight attached to each factor. This weight should be a measure which according to your judgement shows how important that factor is in making a choice.
    In this case, the table shows that A-level points were considered to be weighty evidence. Its relative weight was determined to be 60%.

Using the system

4   Take each choice in turn and for each factor enter the appropriate grade for that factor. For example, in this case, the first candidate was assigned 100 percentage points for her A-level grades, 10 percentage points for an evaluation of her work experience, 50 percentage points on the basis of the factors evaluated in the interview and 100 percentage points for the support given by the references.

5   For each choice make the following sets of calculations:

    (i) For each factor multiply the grade by the weight, to give you the net amount.

    (ii) Add the net amounts for each factor to get the total for that choice.
        For example, in this case, the first candidate gets a net amount of 60 points for A-levels (60% of 100 is 60), 1 point for work experience (10% of 10), 10 points for the interview (20% of 50) and 10 points for the references (10% of 100); the candidate's score is, therefore, 60+1+10+10 = 81.

A table embodying a subjective linear system.

Applicant	A levels 60%		Work Exp 10%		Interview 20%		References 10%		Total 100%
	grade	net	grade	net	grade	net	grade	net	score:
1	100	60	10	1	50	10	100	10	81
2	60	36	100	10	100	20	50	5	71
3	40	24	10	1	100	20	80	8	53
998	40	24	100	10	100	20	100	10	64
999	60	36	50	5	100	20	100	10	71
1000	80	48	0	0	60	12	20	2	62

In the example, the score of each applicant is an estimate of how well the system predicts the applicant will do on the course. This forecast is used to make a decision on whether to admit a candidate.

The benefits

A subjective linear system will work well as long as you include all the important factors. The system illustrated above could be improved upon. In these days of APL and APEL the model looks decidedly thin. But the virtue of constructing a linear system is that doing so forces you to think deeply about your decisions – that is the point of constructing a system. You should:

- think deeply about the factors that are important;

- think about how to give grades on each factor, and how to ensure consistency;

- think about which factors are the most important, and assign relative weights.

If you do this vital work in setting up a linear system you are likely to have thought deeply about the decision and are more likely to get a good decision. It is a relatively simple matter to do the calculations, especially using a spreadsheet. The spreadsheet is not important, the thinking and preparation behind are.

Objective linear systems

If you make the same class of decision frequently, and if the data on the outcomes of the decisions are available, and if you have no reason to think that there are new significant factors, then you can perform better than the subjective linear model. The construction of the system is the same, except that you infer the weights statistically from the results.

3.8 The consensual approach to decision making

It is often said that a group should try to reach a consensus. It is not often clear what this means in practice and the lack of clarity can lead to the making of poor decisions with low-level commitment. A truly consensual approach to decision making tends to produce good-quality decisions with a high level of commitment.

A mistaken assumption

There is an assumption that a group of intelligent people must come up with good choices. This assumption is an error. Acting on the assumption will lead you to frustration. Groups are liable to come to a consensus too quickly, focus on evidence which confirms their opinions, and preserve group cohesiveness through conformity.

The extra need of a group

A group should be especially careful to explicitly address the various aspects of the decision-making process (see § 3.1) as it harder for a group to change direction. In addition to this, a group must ask what the role of the group is in each aspect or phase, as it is possible that the group needs to function differently in each one.

The meaning of 'consensual'

A consensual approach to decision making does not mean that the goal is to secure unanimity of decision. A consensual approach is one which emphasises creating options, discussion of options, identifying goals, revealing values and learning. A consensual approach to decision making is highly interactive and tends to produce good-quality decisions with a high level of commitment. Each individual should be able to accept the group's decision on the basis of its soundness and feasibility. A consensual approach aims to secure a decision which everyone can live with.

- Conflict is a natural outcome of strongly held positions. It should not be avoided. Everyone, however, has a responsibility to contain it. Do not assume that one party must win and one party must lose. Instead, look to your goals and interests (treat the discussion like a negotiation, see § 6.6 Principled negotiation).

- Do not use, and encourage others not to use, avoidance techniques such as voting and bargaining. Do not let someone get the idea that they are 'owed one' if they yield on a point. No one should change their mind solely on the basis of avoiding conflict or as a bargaining chip. Check the reasons why each member of your group accepts the decision.

- Focus on goals rather than positions. Encourage others to focus on goals too. In argument try to clarify the goals and separate out your position. Do not yield merely because someone thinks they have a veto. Actively listen to their position and seek common ground before you say where you disagree. Argue hard on goals, soft on position.

Listening

In a group meeting, when there is disagreement and things are not moving ahead, suggest that everyone makes their position clear.

Take a flip-chart and write across the top a scale.

For	4 3	2 1	1 2	3 4	Against

- List the members names down one side.
- Ask each person to state their position of the scale.
- Indicate this on the chart.
- Suggest that those who are strongly for the position to explain the views of those against it.

33

- Suggest that those who are strongly against the position to explain the views of those for it.

Not only does this encourage active listening, it gets the reasons out in the open quickly.

Management of group decisions

In routine or ritualistic decision making, the chair should give a lead and consensus may quickly follow. In other sorts of decision making, however, the leader should avoid giving her ideas first, she should encourage new ideas and criticism and ensure the group listens to minority views. The purpose is to generate as many ideas as possible and take into account as many goals as possible.

Setting ground rules

Behaviour at meetings is based on assumptions about what is proper. As academics attend many types of meetings, deal with these assumptions by setting ground rules. For example:

(a) Our meetings begin on time.

(b) Members help to set the agenda.

(c) Decisions are made by consensus.

(d) Conflict is acceptable and expressions of feelings and opinions encouraged.

(e) Any member of the group can call 'time out' to stop the discussion to talk about the process or have a break.

Ground rules can be about anything to do with the meeting, about content, structure, procedures and interaction.

4 Action planning

To be effective you need to make things happen. For this you need an 'action plan', a convenient short summary of what has to be done. The better the quality of the action plan, the more likely it is that things will happen and proceed smoothly and successfully. This chapter promotes action planning through discussion of its various aspects. The ideas are presented in terms of team action planning, but any major task you undertake should be treated in this way also and for the same reasons. Action planning is a key component of turning goals into actions and achievements.

4.1 Turning goals into actions

To be effective you need to turn goals into actions. A group works together best when the task is decomposed into smaller tasks and roles are assigned to its members. This section illustrates the processes.

Goals

A department decided to have greater employer involvement as one of its goals; this was defined as 'Improve employer involvement in teaching, planning and monitoring'. A member of staff was given the role of team leader. Three other staff agreed to join the team. In the first meetings the team agreed on three main targets: the criteria of success, the tasks to be undertaken and time-scales, and how to check progress.

Targets and criteria

1   To improve employer involvement within the forthcoming academic year.

Success criteria:
Degree of improvement in the academic year, compared with the previous years, to be judged through analysis of teaching activities supported by employers, the number of employers involved in course review, and the increase in the variety of types of employer involvement.

2   A written policy on employer involvement.

Success criterion:
The policy should be of high quality (e.g., meeting an objective standard) and written by half-term in the first term.

3   The policy should command the support of staff, employers and students.

Success criterion:
The degree to which the policy is accepted and in place by the end of the year.

Tasks and progress checks

The team next considered tasks and progress checks for each target.

For target 1, the best test of acceptance by employers would be the degree of improvement in involvement. Appropriate progress checks were agreed.

For target 2, to get a better idea of what an effective policy might look like, it was agreed that one member of the team would attend a conference ran by the Royal Society. All four would visit similar departments which had better employer involvement, to discuss policy and practice. The director of the Enterprise Unit would be asked to comment on the first draft in the light of her knowledge of what worked elsewhere. Dates for meetings were agreed, and progress checks planned for each of the tasks.

For target 3, getting the policy agreed, it was decided to devote a full session of the staff conference to the issue, with employers involved after the break. Staff agreed to explain and discuss the proposed policy with students in their classes before it was finalised. A departmental meeting would be asked to adopt the policy formally. A member of the team would write for the department newsletter an article which included the views of an employer commending the policy. How far the policy genuinely commanded the support of staff would be gauged before its formal adoption, by informal discussions over coffee between team members and named members of staff; the views would be pooled at a subsequent team meeting.

Initial tasks

Finally, at the planning stage, the team looked at preparations and readiness checks and drew up an action plan for the work, with dates for completion.

Summary

Writing a plan is relatively easy: the difficult part is writing a plan that not only get to grips with the real needs of the department, but is also workable in practice and produces the benefits it sets out to achieve. For this, the planning process needs to be right. It needs to be a learning process.

Action Plan

Goal: To improve employer involvement in teaching, planning and monitoring.

Target 1:   Improve employer involvement by the end of the year.
            Success criterion: Greater number and variety of contacts.

Target 2:   Produce a written policy by the middle of the first term.
            Success criteria: (i) quality (decide criteria later);
                              (ii) on schedule

Target 3:   Policy should command support of staff, employers and students.
            Success criterion: Degree of acceptance by staff, employers and students.

Team: Dr Smith (leader), Dr Jones, Dr Davies, Dr Brown, Dr Green

Time: Progress checks – by all at each meeting.
            Success checks – Dr Smith, end of term 2.

Resources:

(a)   Conference attendance for one team member.
(b)   Time and expenses for visits to similar departments.
(c)   A full session in the staff conference.

Initial tasks:

(a)   Book and attend a conference run by the Royal Society (Dr Smith).
(b)   Identify departments to visit; arrange visits (Dr Jones).
(c)   Book and plan a session in the staff conference (Dr Brown).
(d)   Plan article in newsletter (Dr Green).

Tasks:

(a)   Visit departments (as many as possible).
(b)   Decide success criteria on quality of policy (all).
(c)   Draft policy (Dr Smith to take load).
(d)   Obtain the Enterprise Units view on the quality of the policy (Dr Brown).
(e)   Prepare for the staff conference (Dr Jones and Dr Brown).
(f)   Check acceptability of policy (all).
(g)   Present policy to staff (Dr Smith).
(h)   Present policy to students (all staff, briefed by Dr Brown).
(i)   Write article for newsletter (Dr Green).
(j)   Gain support to implement policy (all).
(k)   Collect evidence (all).
(l)   Collate evidence and make comparisons with previous records (Dr Davies).
(m)   Editing the final report (Dr Smith and Dr Davies).

4.2 Constructing an action plan

Turning general goals into action plans means working out how to implement them and monitor the success in implementation. In practice, goals can be broken down into a range of targets. In devising targets, the group should ensure that every member contributes to at least one task and that no one is involved in too many tasks.

Action plans

An action plan is a working document which describes briefly the programme of work to be undertaken on a particular goal. It contains:

- The goal statement.

- The specific targets for the goal.

- The success criteria which specify outcomes and the standard to be expected.

- The tasks to be undertaken to reach each target.

- The time-lines and allocation of responsibility for targets and tasks.

- The dates for meeting for progress and success checks.

- The resource implications (materials and equipment, finance, training, etc.)

Preparing for evaluation

Setting targets only makes sense if you also have a clear idea of what is to count as success in achieving them. Thinking about the success criteria helps you to define the targets; thinking about the targets helps you to define the success criteria.

The success criteria also provide the basis of the success checks that will be carried out as the work proceeds. Evaluation of what you have achieved needs to go on all the time, not just at the end. It is not simply a matter of finding out, afterwards, whether you hit bull's-eye. You need to know, as you go along, whether your preparations were sound and whether you are on the right track and within the time-frames.

Success criteria

Answering the question: 'Has the quality of our provision and students' learning got better as a result of our efforts?' should suggest the standard you hope to achieve and the evidence you will require in order to be sure that the targets have been reached, in full or in part.

Drafting an action plan

The targets are broken down into concrete tasks for groups or individuals within a chosen time-frame. You need to plan progress checks at this time. They should occur at various points during the life of the project. Progress checks will allow you to assess whether tasks are being completed, standards met and schedules observed, they will also help you to see where change is needed to overcome unexpected obstacles.

Finance, materials, training, etc., must be on hand, or planned to be in place at the appropriate time. These need to be identified and scheduled. You will then be in a position to write the plan down, listing the various jobs in the order in which they will have to be done.

4.3 Performance indicators and success criteria

Indicators

An indicator is a measure that points to something else which is significant, but harder to measure.

Performance indicators

A performance indicator is an easily obtained measurement, which can do duty for professional judgement on the actual performance. These quantitative measures are rarely sufficient as definitive answers to the really important questions.

For example, examination results may be taken as a performance indicator of how well you teach. They say where students have got to a particular subject at particular times. They do not show, however, how far they have progressed, how hard it was for them to get there, or why they have not got further.

Evaluation of the data

Despite their shortcomings performance indicators draw your attention to issues that deserve a closer look. Comparisons between one year and another, between subjects, or between your results and local and national norms should prompt you to ask:

• Are we doing as well as we expected?

• Are we doing as well as others?

• If not, what needs to be done to change the circumstances, and who needs to do it?

Success criteria

The success criteria are similar to performance indicators but are used in goal setting. They are distinctive in that they:

• Refer to future rather than past performance.

• Relate to a planned target designed to improve performance.

• Are chosen by the people who set the target.

• Influence the way the target is designed.

When goal setting, framing success criteria is a vital step in turning goals into actions and is a necessary condition for the ability to learn from the planning activity.

Benefits from the use of indicators

In the context of planning, indicators and success criteria can exert a positive influence on your ways of thinking and your ways of working. They can:

• Promote desirable targets for your goals.

• Suggest standards appropriate to such targets.

• Guide you to achieve agreed standards.

• Indicate the evidence needed to judge success.

• Shape further action, if the degree of success falls short of your expectation.

• Improve decision making.

4.4 Progress checks and evaluation

A progress check is an act of evaluation in the course of activity. It provides an opportunity for a re-orientation.

Checking progress

At least once, a team's progress on each task should be formally checked against the success criteria associated with the target. The team needs clear evidence of progress. If such evidence is recorded, the workload is reduced later.

Regular progress checks involve:

- giving somebody responsibility for ensuring that the progress checks take place;

- reviewing progress at team meetings, especially when taking the next step forward or making decisions about future directions;

- deciding what will count as evidence of progress in relation to the success criteria;

- recording the evidence and conclusions for later use.

Progress checks may show that:

- the time-frames were too tight;

- circumstances have changed since the plan was constructed;

- there is a loss of direction and some corrective is required for the target to be hit.

Checking success

Success checks take place on the completion of the work on a target. The team decides how successful they have been against their success criteria (see the previous section). Checking success need not be complex or time consuming. It will consist largely in collating, and then drawing a conclusion about, the earlier progress checks.

A success check means:

- giving somebody responsibility for collating the progress checks;

- allowing time for the team to discuss and analyse the extent of the success;

- noting changes in practice as a result of the plan;

- working out the implications for future work;

- writing a brief report on each target attempted;

- collating these reports to create a final report, with indications of what helped and what hindered progress to the goal;

- assessing the implications for the department as a whole.

Reporting

The success check provides the basis on which others may be informed, through a newsletter or at an open day for example. Reporting to students should not be forgotten. They play an active role in implementing the plan and have an interest in the outcomes.

4.5 Planning as learning

Innovations create new working conditions where you are called upon to learn from your experience (see § 3.2 Turning experience into learning). In the context of planning and evaluation consider the following points.

Benefits

The benefits of turning planning into learning are that it:

- allows better success checks to be formulated and executed in other exercises;

- makes it easier to report appropriately the outcomes of a plan;

- enhances decision making;

- synergistically combines the professional development of the individual member of staff with the development of the department;

- provides ways of looping the department's internal monitoring and evaluation with the monitoring and evaluation of the others.

Enhancing learning

- Establishing standards is essential. You need to agree on what counts as success.

- Discussion balances your judgement of the progress made towards a particular target against the judgements of others. The grounds of your judgement should be questioned and talked through.

- Reflection on your professional practice, aided by taking a view from a standpoint provided by informed opinion, from books, journals, reports, or the experiences of other staff, is a necessary condition of learning.

- You can ground discussion of your experiences by designing appropriate check sheets (see § 3.3 Check sheets) and arranging mutual observation (in lectures, say) or review of materials (study guides, etc.), as part of a team approach or as an aspect of appraisal. All parties can benefit.

Other data collection may help you:

- Semi-structured interviewing of students.

- Gathering students' reactions, through discussion, written work or a questionnaire. The response should be documented.

- Examination of samples of students' written work by a small team of staff. This may draw attention to the impact of changes in the curriculum or in assessment strategy.

- Tabulated results from student assessment, including routine test scores, examination results, profiles and records of achievement.

- Statistical information collected for the department's own use or for the external bodies.

4.6 Working together in teams

As we are increasingly asked to work together to handle rapid change, and greater demands for accountability, it is worthwhile thinking more deeply what it is to work together in teams and the benefits of doing this. This section helps you to do that thinking.

Benefits of collaboration

There are many benefits from collaboration with other members of staff.
In particular, it:

- creates a commitment to a common purpose

- improves communication and reduces misunderstanding;

- fosters creativity in finding solutions to problems;

- enhances motivation and makes the task more enjoyable;

- prevents individuals from becoming isolated;

- generates a sense of collective achievement;

- encourages other sorts of teamwork.

The keys to effective collaboration

There are various keys to working together successfully. We need to:

- clarify the key responsibilities;

- value the distinctive contributions of each individual;

- recognise that for some tasks horizontal teams (across subjects, departments and year groups) or diagonal teams (as horizontal but drawing from different levels) may be more creative than 'vertical' ones in the department;

- seek agreement about priorities (see Chapter 3 Decision making).

Fostering collaboration

Collaboration is fostered when we:

- are open about the planning and management of change;

- give planning the time and status it needs;

- draw upon the diversity of experience, talents and ideas of others;

- are interested in learning from experience.

The team leader's role

The team leader has a key role in co-ordinating the work and in promoting team working. She should ensure that:

- members understand what needs to be done, the time-scale involved and who is to do what;

- members feel that they have a unique contribution to make and that their talents are well used;

- there is a climate of trust and mutual respect among members;

- members discuss various options and approaches to solutions before taking decisions;

- the free expression of ideas, suggestions, doubts, fears and reservations is encouraged;

- there are established ways of working together which make efficient use of people's time;

- progress is checked regularly and members know when, how and to whom they should report.

4.7 Making team meetings effective

Meetings need not always be very formal occasions at which a team discusses business prepared on the basis of an agenda, with supporting papers. A short discussion between two or three staff over coffee at a break is also a form of meeting and it can be just as valuable. Try not to let the tone and style of the meeting be set by chance. Be active in setting the tone and style of any meetings being set up, the meetings you attend, and the meetings you are asked to chair.

Improving meetings

* Encourage informal meetings. If a meeting is formal try to ascertain if there are good reasons for its being so.

* Make sure that your group has, from the beginning, very clear terms of reference and ensure that these are discussed. Doing this raises appropriate expectations and helps to keep discussion to the point.

* Ask for meetings to be as small as possible: the larger the meeting the more difficult it is to fix times when all will be present.

* Suggest appropriate membership – those who can best contribute to the task. Suggest that it is a matter of communication later, for those who need to know about the outcomes of the meeting.

* Suggest the most appropriate person to chair the meeting – not necessarily the most senior member.

* Ask for a fixed finishing time before you start. This concentrates the mind on the business, inhibits diversions and prevents the meeting dissolving because of early departures.

* Where minutes need to be kept, ask for an explicit decision as to what needs to be recorded and reported; ask that the minutes be short (and clear) ones.

* Ask for an 'action column' in the minutes to record who is going to do what before the next meeting.

* Ask for a distribution list to be compiled so that minutes go only to those who need to know or are known to be interested.

* If the location and furniture arrangement are not appropriate to the kind of meeting required, suggest a better alternative.

* When a meeting has to report to a larger meeting, check that the meetings are timed to fit carefully into the cycle.

5 Reading and writing

A large part of academic life is reading and writing, both published and unpublished material, for purposes of study and communication with colleagues. It is no small matter to improve any part of the processes involved. The sections in this chapter suggest possible improvements and give helpful information and advice.

5.1 Planning publications

Publication is not merely for the dissemination of your results, it is part of the formative assessment of your efforts and as such a valuable tool for self-development and the sharpening of your ideas. More deeply it is what creates a wide community of enquirers and drives the acquisition of knowledge forward. Publishing is best not left to chance and should be considered as an integral part of your research and scholarly activities. As such it is worthy of some organisational effort and at least rudimentary planning.

What is a publishing plan?

- A publishing plan, at its simplest, is an annotated list of work you would like to publish, with whom and where.

- At its most elaborate, it is a tool for focusing your research and the dissemination of its results. In this case, a plan will include or be associated with a database of the various means of and outlets for dissemination and a catalogue of your references and publications. It is also a resource that can be used in supporting research training and supervision.

Defining the outlets for work in your area

- Write yourself a short review or overview of research in your area, broadly defined, stating the issues that are important and giving references to landmark papers and major sources.

- Write up a short description of the research you are pursuing, giving a few recent references.

- Make an inventory of the journals you publish in, read, or scan, and those that are frequently referenced in papers you read. Start to compile data on the journals.

- What sort of papers do they favour?

- Who of the referees do you know?

- What are the submission requirements and house style? (If you have a word-processor you can then create appropriate style sheets to be used when writing a paper for that outlet.)

- Which conferences have you given papers at?

- Which conferences have you attended? Why?

- Which conference proceedings do you read?

- What sort of papers do they tend to favour?

- Who on the programme committee do you know?

- What are the submission requirements?

- When, typically, is the conference held?

- What are the important critical dates for submission, etc.?

Maintain your data

- Make sure you are on the appropriate mailing lists.

- Join the appropriate societies.

- Annually update your data and your reviews and overviews.

- Have a list of names and addresses appropriate for this purpose.

Catalogue

It is useful to make your references database state whether you have a copy of the book or article and to record its Dewy number or other library reference. Annotate the reference. If you have an electronic reference database you can create a catalogue of your material by constructing what is called in the terminology of databases a view or layout of the data. Construct your own key word index and put key words with your annotations (see § 5.5 Reading articles.)

Make notes about the information services provided

Keep all your information about your library and information services in one place. Summarise the main points and procedures and keep this summary with your data. Add helpful notes as you go along (e.g. the name and number of the librarian who is the specialist in your area).

5.2 You as a writer

This section is about you as a writer and not about the methods of writing a good paper.

Writers' workshops

Learned societies cannot meet your needs as a writer. Consider encouraging the founding of a local, intimate, supportive group which run writers' workshops. Your group may have a very tightly defined core purpose but encourage informal meetings outside of the main activities. One writing group, for example, also runs occasional 'reading parties' where the members schedule time over a weekend to read separately and discuss collectively an important work by an outsider. As part of the weekend they often schedule dining together, and so on. You may be able to encourage some of your colleagues to form a private group of people who run workshops.

In the workshops you undertake to give each other constructive criticism and support. You meet regularly to discuss academic matters and pieces of writing by the members. One of the main purposes of a writers' workshop is, of course, to improve your published writing, but there is no reason to exclude on principle such things as memoranda, slides and so on.

Make sure you have explicit ground rules for the group which cover such things as the scope of its activities and proceedings.

Benjamin Franklin's Juno Club had, among others, the following rules:

Questions to be answered at every meeting

- Have you met with anything in the author you last read, remarkable, or suitable to be communicated to the Juno?
- What new story have you lately heard agreeable for telling in conversation?
- Have you lately heard any member's character attacked, and how have you defended it?
- Do you see anything amiss in the present customs or proceedings of the Juno, which might be amended?

There were twenty-four questions. To be a member of Juno one had to swear explicitly to four statements of belief, one of which was:

Do you think that any person ought to be harmed in his body, name, or goods, for mere speculative opinions? *Answer.* No

---

Publishing

In collaborative writing you should ask the question "Who should be first author on this paper?" Make sure you answer this question before you start. In default of an explicit agreement to the contrary, custom and practice in many disciplines dictate that the first author is the person who originally formulated the concept and was responsible for the study, regardless of the contributions of others subsequently. This is the best starting-point for a discussion.

A useful practice exercise is for you and a few colleagues to try and decide on a method which would rank author's names on a paper. As a starter you might consider the following criteria: conceptual input, planning, hours of time doing the research, data collecting, data analysis, preparation of draft, final editing, years since getting a doctorate, academic rank, administrative support.

Acknowledgements

You should acknowledge all those who have contributed to the research, writing or publication. It is a sad fact that people do not fully recognise the contributions of others and it is best that you err on the side of generosity. Your acknowledgements, however, should be simple and sincere.

Referees

The reports of referees are often ambiguous and are occasionally wrong. But you lose if you ignore them. Take referees' comments as valuable clues and investigate them thoroughly. You need not slavishly follow every recommendation, but revise your typescript. If you cannot accept a major criticism from a referee you should explain, clearly and dispassionately, in a letter to the editor why you do not accept it.

A bad report is a fact of life and you should attempt to take it in your stride. If you get serious criticisms more than once by different referees and editors these cannot be dismissed. Launch a deep review of what you are doing and why. Try to involve your reference group (see § 7.7). You may even have to ask yourself fundamental questions. Am I building on strength? What are my goals?

If you have a paper rejected it is always an option to improve it in the light of referees' comments and submit it to another journal. A second rejection means you should forget that paper. Editorial boards can form quite tight circles and you should not be seen to be hawking a paper around for too long.

Large publications

Writing large works has an enormous impact on your other work and family. Think carefully about undertaking such a task. Writing is a difficult, time-consuming business. It is hard to keep your motivation and to be disciplined about it. You will need all your organisational skills and as much support as you can get. It is such a difficult task that many would-be authors prefer to work with another, for support and company.

Commercial publishers are not charitable organisations. Throughout negotiations, consult colleagues who have published a few books and take their advice.

5.3 Page makeup

One way to help people read your writing is to improve the format of your text. Doing this not only helps your reader: the mechanics of writing are made easier if you have a standard format with which you become familiar.

Use a simple basic format

Unless you have specific reasons to deviate from a basic format stick to it. Many word-processing packages allow you construct 'styles' and 'stationery' in which you can express your fundamental settings and create versions for different types of documents. It is worth looking up these things in the manual. Schedule time to construct a set of styles and find out the quick ways to apply them.

Good page design

- For the text body use a good serif typeface (like Times Roman).

- For the headings use a sans serif bold typeface (Helvetica is standard).

- Have no more than 65 characters per line (5.6 inches wide in Times 12 point).

- Use a print area of 1.6:1 for pleasing proportions. (These guidelines mean that, on A4 paper using Times 12 point, the text area should be about 8.8 x 5.6 inches. You can get near this by setting your margins as follows: top, 1 inch; bottom, 1.2 inches; right, 0.75 inches; left, 2 inches).

General

- Do not justify the text.

- Set headings as sentences with capital initials on the first word and proper nouns only.

- Remember that CAPITALS, *italics*, and <u>underlined</u> text are harder to read.

- In all documents allow white space in the text: make paragraphs seven or eight lines long at the most.

Memoranda

- One A4 page at most. Otherwise treat as a short report with covering memo.

- Give a subject matter or benefit statement as an opener.

- Highlight actions and give dates.

- Use a simple written style, close to telegraphic.

Letters

- Wider margins (add 0.3 inches to the margins).

- Add headline and sub-headings.

- Use bullets and numbered lists.

- Print your title, name and role below your signature.

Reports

- Make the title meaningful.

- Construct a table of contents and make it explanatory.

- Make an executive summary and spend a lot of time on writing it.

- Use headings and sub-headings.

- Open with 'topic sentences' which build on sub-headings.

- Give a graphical emphasis where possible.

- Give captions to charts, tables, diagrams and illustrations.

5.4 Proof-reading

It is best to think of authoring as having distinct phases: writing, proof-reading and printing. Proof-read a draft as an explicit procedure. The following systematic procedure makes proof-reading easier and more effective.

Preliminaries

- Schedule your proof-reading time and treat is as an explicit task.

- When you have finished writing, do not proof-read straight away. Leave it until a scheduled time, preferably the next day. Proof-read for no more than 20 minutes at a time.

- Attach a proof-reading checklist to the draft and tick off items as you go along. Note on the check list, or a post-it note, where you have left off. Date, time and filename the document.

First phase

- Read for sense.

- Proof-read headers, footers, names.

- Check quotes and brackets for opening and closing pairs.

- Check numbering of sections and pages.

- Check hyphens.

- If you have a tendency to make egregious errors (e.g. mixing whose/who's, its/it's, there/their/they're, you/your/you're, to/too/two, principal/principle, etc.) then note them and make up a rule or mnemonic that will distinguish the right one ('the principal is my PAL'). Until you get them right, check for these errors as a separate, first, pass and mark the corrections.

Second phase

- Mechanically check spellings and punctuation. Mark the text. Don't do the corrections.

- Look up the facts: e.g. 'In section 3, we . . . .'.

- Check the table of contents.

- Make a list of queries you must address before finishing the text: e.g. 'C. S. Peirce or C. S. Pierce?'

Final phase

- Give the text a final read.

- Make corrections and print out a clean copy.

- Check corrections made against draft and query sheet.

It has been found that there are more errors in beginnings, at the end of lines; errors tend to occur in groups; people often miss errors in familiar short words (e.g. 'tha' for 'the'). Justified text is harder to read than unjustified, and you have to be more careful with it.

Techniques:

- Read with a rule.

- Read out loud.

- Mark up text and margins with proof-correcting symbols (see the box below).

- Those who are poor at spotting things will need other aids: read from bottom to top, right to left; fold the page and 'read' each half, as though it were a column.

- Use different coloured inks for marking up and checking off.

A basic set of proof-correcting symbols

Correction	Text markings	Marginal note	Correction	Text markings	Marginal note
Insert (the symbol for space is #)	Mark the place by the up stroke of ⋏	Write the material followed by ⋏	Ignore all or part of corrections	Write......dots under material to remain as was	*stet*
Delete	Draw a line through the material	ᓑ	Make bold	Write a wavy line under letter/s	*Bold*
Substitute new material for marked text	Draw a line through the material	Write new material followed by /	Make italic	Write line under letter/s	*Ital.*
Transpose letters or words	⌐way⌐this	*trs*	Insert new paragraph	word⌐ Word	*n.p.*
Close up	g⌒ap	⌒	Delete paragraph break	word. ⌐ Word	*run on*
Superior insert, for any character x	⌄x/	⌄	Make capital letters	Write three lines under letter/s ≡	*cap*
Inferior insert, for any character x	/⌄x	⌄	Make lower case letters	Encircle letter/s ⌀	*l.c.*

If you use a word-processor, use the spell-checker but do not think of that as proof-reading. Whatever you do on screen think of as 'writing'. Print a draft and follow your proof-reading procedure. Do not make the corrections until the final phase. After corrections have been made prepare the document for printing.

Involving others

- A normal person only catches around 75% of the errors, so you should use two readers.

- Encourage constructive criticism.

Being an Effective Academic

5.5 Reading articles

Academics read a wide variety of material which calls for a flexibility of approach. Sometimes we need to read actively and this calls for a disciplined approach. As reading is such a major part of our role, it is no trivial matter to give it some explicit attention.

Active reading

An active approach to reading a paper is to make sure that you ask various questions of it and read with a view, *inter alia*, to answering them. Consider the questions below:

- What is the problem or issue addressed?

- What are the major references cited?

- What is their summary or conclusion?

- What do I think the article's strong points are?

- What do I think the article's weak points are?

- What comments would I like to make?

Depending on your discipline, you may consider these questions relevant:

- What method and techniques were used?

- What are the major stages in the work?

- How are the results analysed?

- To what school of thought does the author appear to belong?

Take an active approach to review. Schedule your review periods.

Cataloguing

Consider cataloguing what you read, making your reading objectives, approach and questions to be answered part of the record. This is especially useful if you have an electronic database for your catalogue and you can search freely through it (your database needs to allow 'text fields'). It does not matter if you set up your catalogue with more fields than you typically use, as you can always leave them blank. But having a template for each entry based on the ideas in this section will encourage you to take an active approach to reading.

Group working

If you work with a group do not make your database private, share it and, if your software will enable it, allow others to put in their comments.

Attachments

If you do not keep a catalogue, consider making a standard attachment sheet for each article you file. This standard attachment could be your overview of the paper, based on the answers to the questions above. If you are working in a group, make provision for the attachment to encourage others to make comments on the article.

A reference database table

Author(s)	Title

Journal	Year	Volume	Number	Library reference	Own copy?

Problem or issue: (or key words)	Method:	Results:
School of thought:	Strong points:	Summary:
Stages in the work:	Weak points:	Comments:

Major references cited:

Author(s)	Title
Journal	Year	Volume	Number	Library reference	Own copy?

Author(s)	Title
Journal	Year	Volume	Number	Library reference	Own copy?

Author(s)	Title
Journal	Year	Volume	Number	Library reference	Own copy?

5.6 Reading books

Active reading

In one form or another you probably always sample a book before you read it properly. Make this sampling process more conscious: read the table of contents, skim read the index, the introductions to the chapters and summaries. Find something you are interested in and read that first. If you decide to read the book, answer the following questions and write down the answers:

- Why you are going to read it? (To review it, to get an idea of the contents, for lecturing material, for research, for extending your general knowledge.)

- What approach are you going to take to reading it? (Read the chapters relevant to your concern, read it through with a note pad at hand.)

- What questions would I like to be able to answer when I have read it?

When you have answered these questions, you will read the book much more effectively and efficiently. If your approach involves taking notes, consider taking them in network form (see § 5.7 Note-taking.) Make sure that you have answered all your questions, or know why the book has not answered them, and stop. Take an active approach to review: schedule your review periods.

Organising your library

Establish a system so that you will be able to find books when you need them.

- Divide the books into classes.

- Within each class, if necessary, organise them according to subdivisions.

- Sort alphabetically within each division.

- Take an inventory of the books you want to have readily accessible.

- Decide where to store each division: reference books near your desk, computer manuals near your computer, and so on.

- It is a good idea to place books you use often in plastic racks which take just two or three books in each slot. You can remove and replace them easily without others falling over and without losing the place.

Catalogues

It is useful to have your references state whether you have a copy of the book or article. If you have an electronic reference database you can create a catalogue of your books by construction this view of the data (see § 5.5 Reading articles).

Lending

- Have a hardback notebook and when someone borrows a book from you record their name, the book's title and an agreed date of return. If necessary, record an address or telephone number.

- Put your name and address sticker on the book, to clearly identify you as the owner.

After you have lost quite a few books you learn to be firmer in your refusals to lend.

5.7 Note-taking

The purpose of making notes is review and process. Therefore, notes need to encode information, organise it, and ease the process of making inferences. To do this well, your notes should be organised around key words and key images.

A thematic network expressing the ideas in this section

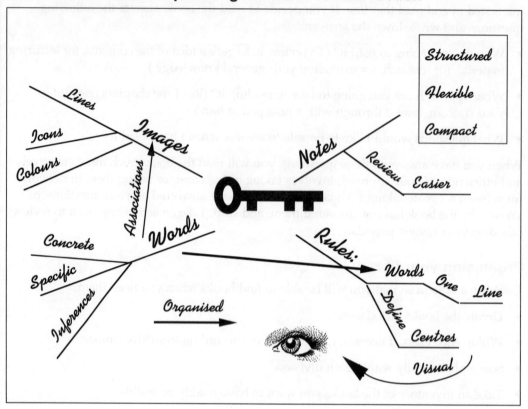

Visual

Thematic networks use icons, images and lines, colour where possible.

Organisation

Putting this encoded information into thematic networks helps you to organise it. Connect your key words and images by links and arrows.

Benefits

Such networks have advantages over ordinary notes. For developing ideas, these types of notes allow you to unfold the subject matter holistically without commitment to specific arguments and textual arrangement.

5.8 Review periods

Repetition and review are essential to memory consolidation. It is more effective and efficient if you establish a system of review whenever you have any material to master.

Your first review of the material should be about five to ten minutes after your study. This short break maximises the so-called 'reminiscence effect' and then a five-minute review is most effective. The second review period should be about a day later, but need only take a couple of minutes. The third review should take place about one week later and take only a couple of minutes. The fourth after about a month and the final one after four months. You could schedule them and post the details to yourself with a Brought Forward file (see § 1.3 Brought Forward file).

Suppose you plan to master the basics of elementary logic, and schedule two sessions of an hour long, each week, over the year.

The structure of each session:

Review of the work on that day a week before	2-3 mins
Review of the work on that day a month before	2-3 mins
Review of the work on that day four months before	2-3 mins
Preview of the day's work (see sections 5.5 and 5.6)	1-3 mins
The day's work	28-43 mins
Complete break, e.g. stretching, juggling, walking	5-10 mins
Review of that session's work	5-10 mins

On the day after a session:

Review of the previous day's work	3-5 mins

Review will be more effective if you take notes with your review needs in mind (see § 5.7 Note-taking).

Do not believe that you are working well simply because you work incessantly at the coalface. Review periods and short breaks greatly increase your effectiveness. To work well you must devote time to satisfying these important psychological needs.

6 People

Education is about people and yet, until recently perhaps, we have rarely addressed the interpersonal skills needed to be a successful academic. In this chapter you will find ideas which you may be able to adopt or adapt. These interesting techniques and skills have been proven to be effective; the mere attempt to put them into practice will make you more effective. Practice and repetition are all that is needed to improve, and you may become highly skilled.

6.1 Planning for an unpleasant interview

We sometimes need to tell tutees, or others, that they cannot do, or have, something they want, or that their performance or behaviour is unsatisfactory in some respect. It is tempting to delay or avoid or fluff doing this, because it is an unpleasant situation.

Before the meeting

1 Brief yourself. This is essential. The other person will try to put aside what you say or use the fact that you are unsure or wrong in some detail as a way of keeping the issue open. You need to know the detailed facts; if you rely on vague generalisations the session will become even more difficult to handle and you will be feel the temptation merely to assert your authority.

2 Determine what you want to be the outcome of the session. For example, you will not want to demotivate the person.

During the meeting

3 Control what you convey by your facial expression and body language. A calm manner that gives the person your undivided attention will show a certain respect and provide reassurance.

4 Open with a short, simple statement which will make absolutely clear what the interview is about. Any lack of clarity at this stage can cause confusion and increase the chances of the session being less than satisfactory. Do not rush. It is important to allow either a silence or an uninterrupted response.

5 Place your discussion in context by referring to what the institutional policy is and what you are trying to achieve. This will help the person to see the rationale of what you are doing and not construe it as a personal attack.

6 Do not rush. You are likely to cause resentment if you do not give ample time to discuss the matter fully.

7 Seek agreement on as many points as you can. One good way to get agreement is to ask for suggestions about an effective way forward and use these as the basis for action. If you do not get expressed agreements the person is likely to leave your office resentful; they are more likely to act on their own suggestions.

8 Do not attack them personally; take care not to undermine their confidence. Talk to them about their actions and behaviour and not about their attitudes and personality traits. If they raise these things, tell them they are not an issue. Tell them what the issue is; do not play the therapist.

9 Summarise what has been agreed and what is now to happen, or has been decided. This is vital in order to make things clear. Do not open any new issues or change the topic, end the session there. Do not dismiss them, stand up and walk them to the door. Make sure you do not undermine what you have said, but make sure that they understand that you know their value and do not feel bad about them personally.

If the session has been about something that is particularly important for them, you should remember that, no matter how reasonable their reaction may be, they will be initially embittered. It is important to have supplied a positive note which can have some value later. Do not expect them to be on their absolutely best behaviour; give a little leeway. If they start to go too far, make sure that they know what is unacceptable.

6.2 Dealing with negative politics

The politics of an organisation can be positive, or at least not destructive. There are times when you have to exercise your influencing skills rather than directly support or oppose a proposal. To do this you have to understand and use the political processes. That, in itself, is not being negative. The negative sense of politics comes from the unprincipled use of these political processes.

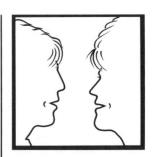

The phenomena

The most pernicious political operators are personally motivated to work behind the scenes, blocking proposals they do not like. They are envious and jealous and act accordingly. They are negative in meetings and bring out the shibboleths such as 'I'm worried about the resource implications,' but they rarely show their hand and prefer to work in the shadows where they cannot be seen easily and can dive for cover if necessary. They spread gossip in the name of 'What I heard', and thus contrive to evade responsibility for what they say.

There are operators who do not know their own motives and would not recognise themselves when reading this description. Their behaviour is overarched by a feeling that they are justified in doing what they do; but that conviction does not make their conduct professional.

Recognise the signs

The signs that operators are at work are well known. They include the following:

* Unexplained and apparently arbitrary delays in decision making.

* Hidden decisions.

* People evading responsibility.

* Excessive lobbying.

* The formation of orchestrated offensives against individuals and groups.

* Memorandum wars.

* Whisper campaigns.

* Snide comments and criticisms.

When you spot this behaviour, find out who the operators are, how they are working, and what they are trying to achieve. In the early stages, direct and open confrontation can put an end to the campaign. It is not always possible to do this; political activity can unsettle those with formal authority, who may take the easy option and suppress anything which threatens them.

How should you behave?

The best course of action is, whenever you can, to bring the issue into the open. Do not give in to the temptation to fight back with the same political weapons (even though one of the operator's tactics may be to say that you are politicking). Do not lie or shade the truth (even though one of the operator's tactics may be to call you a liar). When you are baited, never respond without thinking through the correct principles and only act, when you are sure of them. It is best not to take the bait. When things have gone on for too long, or the political forces are very powerful, to fight on their ground can become dangerous for you, your department and the organisation.

Do not let negative politics sap your self-confidence and foster self-doubt. Evaluate what has happened or is happening to see what you can learn from it. Do not get even. That is a pastime of the weak and insecure and a waste of time and energy. To hate and resent your so-called enemies damages your health, exhausts you, and ruins your looks. Get absorbed in something bigger. Appraise your strengths and continue to build on them.

61

6.3 Helping to create a positive environment

Best professional practice is demanding and these demands are best faced in a positive environment. You can help to create and sustain a positive environment by realising that you can and do make a difference. This section discusses several things you can aspire to do.

Dealing with complaints

Some people moan as a way of life. No matter what you do they will find fault. Some criticism comes from people who are supportive and professional; if you can prevent yourself from being defensive about their criticism, you may find a path to something genuinely valuable. Sometimes criticism is just letting off steam and is not really about what is irritating them.

Do not take criticism as a personal insult (even if you think you know it is intended as such). Listen actively with your full attention. Active listening means showing that you really hear what is being said. Repeat back what you have gathered from the criticism, adding your evaluation of the critic's feelings. 'So you feel you have been slighted because . . .?' Do what you can to solve the problem, even if you think it is trivial. If you have made a mistake admit it.

Keep your temper

Arguing is an unproductive waste of time and energy. The best way to win an argument is to avoid it. Do not try to force your point of view down someone's throat. It is not necessary to agree with them either. If someone disagrees with you, as often as not you can let it pass. Even when your work demands that you have to settle your differences, there is no call for argument. Deal with disagreement through active listening. After they accept that you understand, find and build on common ground and show where you can agree. Then, and only then, point out where you don't agree. It is probably never a good idea to flatly contradict someone. If you have discussed the situation thoroughly, don't make matters worse by going on and on. Instead, refer to someone whose judgement you both respect.

Correcting the mistakes of others

Do not overlook mistakes, but don't think your task is to humiliate the person concerned. Discuss the mistake without fuss. Be as pleasant as you can and try to understand the cause of the mistake, and how to prevent its happening again. Treat others as professionals who want to prevent mistakes as much as you do.

Keeping confidences

Some colleagues find it impossible to keep a confidence. They like to be 'in the know'. Professionals know better. If you betray a confidence, and it gets back, and it will get back, you will forfeit trust completely. Even if something was not said to you in confidence, you should consider it so and ask explicitly whether you may pass it on to others. It is especially important, and difficult, to keep a confidence when a rumour is flying round. Do not confirm or deny a rumour without the explicit permission of the person concerned. There are no good reasons for not keeping a confidence. If you feel you cannot, or should not, keep a confidence, you should not accept it. Say that you are sorry but you do not want to hear it.

Avoiding destructive behaviour

Some staff are not content to run their own affairs; they want to run everyone else's too. They criticise people and procedures and gossip about problems. They are deadly. Their kind of talk leads to friction. Rumours get started and feelings get hurt. These people are not necessarily trying to be destructive. They may be most sincere and really believe that so-and-so is this-and-that, or that things really are badly wrong. But sincerity does not help. The behaviour still leads to friction and bitterness.

Professionals not only do not engage in this behaviour, they try to sustain an environment in which it does not flourish. If you have a problem, point it out in a direct way to the proper person (or, if you feel you really must avoid the direct approach, use the proper procedures). Do not get into the habit of letting off steam in public. Convey to those who do that, unless all the facts are known, it is only fair not to be so negative. Also, convey to them that even if the criticism is completely accurate, it still isn't proper to gripe in public.

Handling your moods

Emotional ups and downs can be a problem. When you are down you see things in a poor light. A bad mood can cause you to make bad decisions, hurt people's feelings, or analyse a situation incorrectly. To guard against bad moods the first thing to do is to become aware of them. Admit to yourself, 'I am in a bad mood.' When you are aware of a bad mood, and admit it to yourself, you are more likely to make allowances for it. If your mood has got a very tight grip, then you should be aware that your judgement will be affected and you should delay taking action or making decisions until you are feeling less negative.

No matter how you feel, try to act in a reasonable way. Further, when lecturing or meeting students try to smile. Your emotions can 'set' your face in a negative expression and it may help if, before you meet others, you consciously loosen up the muscles by facial exercises. You may feel silly with a smile on your face, but you will not look it. Smiling puts people at ease and it catches on. If you get into the smiling habit you will help morale.

Being a colleague

There are many factors involved in being a good academic, but academics share certain attitudes with everyone who does a good job. In the first place, they are interested in their job. They think that what they do is important. Secondly, they think of themselves as distinct individuals, and that what they do makes a difference. Third, they are proud of what they do. They know that the way they do their job reflects their character and they want to do it well.

Since these are the attitudes of good academics and since you want to promote your academic interests, you will help to make your department interesting, you will help your colleagues to be proud of their work, and you will treat your colleagues as important individuals.

Being an Effective Academic

6.4 Active listening

If you have ever met someone with poor listening skills you will know how it undermines their effectiveness and causes more work for everyone. To be an active listener is a vital part of being a professional as well as being a good academic.

Not listening

You are not listening if you do any of the following:

- Assume that the responses of your interlocutor are wholly predictable.

- Go on doing something else, even mentally, while they talk.

- Never ask what they mean.

- Cut across what they are saying to rebut or qualify what they are saying.

- Try to change the subject to something that's on your mind.

Not listening is the cause of many wasted hours and much misunderstanding.

To put this right, the first thing to do is listen. Stop what you are doing and give the person your full attention for the purpose of understanding what they want out of the interaction. That is, be attentive, empathetic and patient. Try to understand what they are feeling and acknowledge their emotions. 'I can see you're feeling pleased.' Accept that the other person may need a bit of time to say what they want. Don't jump to conclusions. Go on to listen actively.

Active listening

- Use the other person's name.

- Ask them to explain crucial points or what they mean by certain words.

- Ask open-ended questions which cannot be answered by one or two words. 'Tell me more about . . . .'

- Tell them pertinent things about yourself, especially difficulties and problems you have had. (This encourages them to be open in return.)

- Check whether you have got what they are saying right: 'Let me see if I've understood that last point. Are you saying . . .?'

- Build on their ideas, use their idiom and vocabulary. Say things that refer back to what they have said before.

- Summarise.

Help others to listen

If you think the other person is not listening, ask questions and try to ensure an exchange of information and views. Summarise your position at the end.

6.5 Undertaking delegated tasks

You often work under delegated authority and this causes no problems. However, you may be asked to accept a task that challenges you and calls for thought and creativity. This task might have been carried out by a more senior person normally, but in this instance that person chooses to delegate the task to you. Properly handled, these are the tasks which will fulfil and motivate you.

Seven important points

It is in your interest to ensure that all concerned understand the following points:

1   Ensure that you know why the work needs to be done.

2   Ensure that you know what is expected of you.

3   Ensure that you know a date by which the task is to be completed.

4   Ensure that you know precisely what your authority is for making decisions, and how it is expected you will come to decisions.

5   Ensure that you know the problems which must be referred back.

6   Ensure that you have a reporting structure. Know when progress checks are expected and what the expected form of the final report or recommendation is.

7   Ensure that you know the resources and help available to you.

Try to ensure that you have a time when you go over the final report or recommendation and encourage criticism. You have worked hard on the task and should expect the courtesy of attention and criticism; also by this process you make commitment and support more likely.

If you are unsure of what to do

If the task seems too challenging for you, or you are very unsure how to proceed, do not reject the offer. Make it known that you will need close liaison, at least initially. It is in your interest to be open. Do not be offended if it turns out that it is thought best to assign the task to someone else: volunteer to help that person. If the task comes to you, ensure a reporting structure with frequent progress checks. At one of these, review the reporting structure. Always have an agenda for these meetings, and question and probe.

Raising difficulties

Never go to a meeting expecting merely to be told what to do. You are then effectively giving the job back and wasting the other person's time. For every problem have a note which has the following structure:

- A specification of the problem as precise and concise as possible.

- An analysis of the causes of the problem – the real causes, not an uninformed trotting out of the obvious. (You may have to go back and reformulate the problem statement.)

- Three possible solutions, or approaches to solving the problem, and their pros and cons.

- A recommendation.

If you do this you are very unlikely to be wasting someone else's time and you are in a much better position to learn from their response.

6.6 Principled negotiation

You are a negotiator. It is a fact of life. Negotiation, however, has negative connotations and most of us, on the whole, want to participate without employing tricks and posturing. There is one approach to negotiation that enables you to do this; it is called 'principled negotiation'. The method, developed at Harvard University, is to decide issues on their merits, looking for mutual gains and using independent standards of fairness. Principled negotiation is the natural ally to consensual approaches to decision making (see § 3.8).

The Harvard group discovered the best way to evaluate a proposal in a negotiation. They worked out the implications of this deceptively simple insight in the context of negotiating on merit. Even a cursory grasp of the concept and an elementary employment of it will enable you be a better negotiator.

The core insight of principled negotiation

It is a mistake to think of negotiating power as being determined by resources. In fact, negotiating power depends upon how attractive it is to you not to reach an agreement. Thus, you can strengthen your negotiating power by proper investigation of what you will do if you do not reach an agreement. This is the core insight of principled negotiation.

The standard you should use to evaluate any proposed agreement is one based on a comparison of the proposal with your best alternative to a negotiated agreement (or BATNA, Best Alternative To a Negotiated Agreement). This alternative is the only relevant standard. In negotiation, instead of taking positions and ruling out options, you compare a proposal with your BATNA and see whether it is better in satisfying your interests.

Possible alternatives do not fall from above, you have to develop them. The next two sections give suggestions on how to do this.

Identify your interests

First, identify your interests. Your interests are the needs, desires, concerns or fears which lead you to take a position on what you want. To uncover your interests ask yourself why you want what you want. The point of doing this is that while it may not be possible to get exactly what you expressly wanted when entering the negotiation, it may be possible to satisfy your interests, if you are aware of them.

Develop your alternatives

When you have identified your interests, develop your alternatives:

1   Make a list of actions or options that you think you might conceivably adopt. Consider three types of alternative. First, identify your walk-away alternatives. Second, identify what you can do to make the other party respect your interests. Third, identify how you can bring a third party into the negotiation to further your interests.

2   Take the more promising alternatives, work them out in detail, investigate them further and develop them into practicable alternatives. Apply what you have to effective negotiating power by developing your options.

3   Adopt one as your BATNA. If you are not successful in your negotiation this is the option you will pursue. It is your best way of satisfying your interests without the other's agreement.

The better your BATNA the more power you have, the better your chances of improving on the terms of any proposal, and the greater your willingness not to agree when it is in your interest not to do so. The clarity and confidence brought by identifying your BATNA are invaluable and make you much more able to pursue principled negotiation.

Identify the other's interests and alternatives

Attempt to identify the other party's interests and BATNA. Their BATNA may be better for them than any fair solution. If you each have an attractive BATNA the best outcome for both might be not to reach agreement.

If the other party refuses to play

When a party to a negotiation refuses to play, they typically attack you and your ideas or they forcefully propound their position. A principled negotiator can deal with these attacks.

- If they attack you, recast the attack as a contribution to solving the problem. Listen actively and then identify common ground and things you can agree with. Think of a motive for the attack which is to do with a concern in the problem and take the issue up from that concern. Do not worry about pausing to think.

- If they attack your ideas invite them to elaborate the criticism or ask for their advice. Listen actively. Find out their concerns and try to rework your ideas with those in mind.

- Bargaining over position tends to obscure the opportunity for joint gains. When the other party marks their position, actively listen and look for the interests and principles it covers. Treat their position as one possible option for meeting these interests and go on from there. For any position, treat it as an attempt to solve the problem and examine the extent to which it meets the interests of each party. If it falls short, see if it can be improved upon.

Negotiation on merits

There are four basic aspects of negotiation and these are dealt with in specific ways by those seeking to negotiate on merits.

1 **Separating people from the problem**
   People become entangled with the problem. The principled way of dealing with this is to separate the problem from the people. You should see your colleagues as working on an objective problem and refuse, no matter what your suspicions, to interpret their acts otherwise. Separating the people from the problem makes it possible to deal with others as professionals and increases the chance of an amicable agreement.

2 **Satisfy interests**
   People often state their position on an issue when the real object of negotiation is to satisfy interests. Taking positions obscures what you all really want. You should see the problem as producing an agreement which will effectively take care of the needs of everyone. The more you understand the others' interests the better able you are to satisfy them at a minimum cost.

3 **Devise options**
   While under pressure it is difficult to widen our vision. Schedule time within which you can think up a wide range of possible solutions. You may be able to devise clever ways of meeting everybody's interests. Seek options that advance shared interests and reconcile differing interests.

4 **Use standards**
   You may have a valuable relationship with the other party, and understand their interests, and you may have generated ingenious options, but yet you find the harsh truth is that your interests conflict. In this case, insist that you use some (not necessarily your) fair standard, such as expert opinion, custom, law, which is independent of the will of either side. By focusing on criteria rather than what either party will or will not do, you make it more likely that each party can agree to a fair solution rather than give in.

The principled negotiator is open to reasoned persuasion on the basis of merits but combines this with an insistence on a solution based on objective criteria. A person who adopts this strategy never yields to pressure, only principle. It is these elements that make the principled negotiator persuasive, and in the long run the most effective. They run in a different race from political operators.

Principled negotiating enables you to be fair without being taken advantage of. There are no tricks. The method is generally applicable to both your academic and private life.

6.7 Communication

Talking

Talking to your colleagues is usually more effective than sending memos or messages. You can see their reaction and learn from it; you are less likely to get misunderstanding; you are more likely to get useful feedback; you add personal impact and you form the basis for improving your relationship. This personal touch is a vital element to our professional communication.

The hindsight effect

The personal touch is not sufficient, however, as we must guard against the hindsight effect. The hindsight effect is that events seem inevitable with hindsight. The hindsight effect is one reason why you should record all agreements in writing. Without written records, people come to have different versions of the same agreement when new information arises. This is an unfortunate, but perfectly natural, side effect of the way our minds work. As we abstract and organise information we assimilate it in ways that make it irreversibly integral to what was there before. You cannot think the way you did. Thus, even if colleagues have a strategic motive for remembering differently, if your memories differ, you should not think that they are lying. There is no cure for this condition, only prevention.

Memoranda

Memos should be reserved for formal communication as a matter of record, to confirm agreements after a discussion, to give detailed clarification, and for the circulation of routine information or requests.

These functions of memoranda are, at least unconsciously, understood by most people. You will let go of something in conversation which you would not let go in writing – even if it is not the main point. The more suspicious you are of the motives of the writer the more you feel obliged to answer everything written or implied.Thus, even if a memo is not be the start of a memo war, it can cause everyone to waste time. Memoranda have to be written with a clear objective in mind and be as direct and spare as possible.

Electronic mail

Many working groups consider electronic mail as closer to personal communication than paper memos. For example, people will tolerate in their own and others' electronic messages typos which would be thought egregious errors in memoranda. On the other hand, they will quickly spot someone who uses electronic mail differently and they will react accordingly. It is best to have two or more message formats and backgrounds which distinguish the different purposes of your electronic communications. The formal ones should be written as though they were memoranda.

Telephone calls

Try to schedule telephone calls in a group. Make an outline of what you intend to say. Log all calls. When you are talking to someone face to face, you have no right to assume that whoever is phoning you is more important. You should put the phone on 'do not disturb', divert the calls to an answering machine or ignore it. The most you can do is answer by saying that you are busy right now and can you call them back.

7 Motivation

Motivation is not about having an iron will. It is about having reasons for actions, deciding to act on those reasons, and when doing so avoiding psychological traps.

No amount of positive thinking or 'go for it' attitudes will enable you to do what you have no real reasons to do. On the other hand, having reasons for action will not get you anywhere, if you do not decide to act. And your decisions will not lead to the best actions if you trap yourself in a negative corner.

This chapter enjoins you to build on strength, manage weakness and have a mission. To help maintain your motivation there are sections on keeping going and handling put-downs. As no one is an island, the final section of this chapter asks you to identify your reference group. These are the people who, among other things, are your psychological support.

Being an Effective Academic

7.1 Build on strength

A strength is an ability and a set of attitudes and values, it is not a social advantage. When building your own future, and the future of those around you, unearthing strengths is the most productive thing you can do. Stop wasting time on your weakness: you will increase your productivity by developing a potential strength.

Detecting potential for strength

The following characteristics are there to help you detect potential for strength:

1 What do you long for? Listen to your longings, they are a clue to a potential strength. (Of course, this is not an infallible guide, as you may long for the mere externals of something rather than for its primary mission; in this case longing for it is not an indication of strength.)

2 What do you get a kick out of doing? It is unlikely you have a potential for strength in some area if you don't get a kick out of doing its typical activities. If you are good at something but don't get a kick out of it, then this is not a strength. A strength feels good.

3 What have you learned quickly? A potential for strength is indicated by a desire to get on with it. You feel as though you know what to do. You are self-directed and learn quickly, managing books and experts as a learning resource.

4 Has someone you respect noticed a moment, an episode, of excellence? This is a clue to a potential strength.

5 When are you on automatic? When are you good, and unconscious of any joints in a flow of events? This is a clue to strength.

You will, no doubt, have more than one strength or potential for strength. Choose one. What makes for achievement is the building on strength.

The policy

The policy of building on strength can be a policy for guiding your personal and professional development, a tool for decision making, and a technique for developing those around you.

7.2 Manage weakness

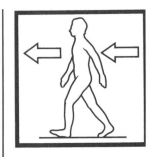

A weakness is something that subverts your productivity and lessens your self-esteem. A weakness must be managed: do not attempt to fix it or turn it into a strength. The point is to manage weakness so that strengths can be developed and the weakness becomes irrelevant.

Recognising weakness

The following characteristics are indicative of weakness:

- You are functioning in an area of weakness when you are defensive. For example, those who are weak in teaching skills blame the students.

- You are slow to learn in an area of weakness.

- You don't grow in an area of weakness. You stop thinking about the future. What you are doing now takes up all your energies.

- When you are functioning in an area of weakness you lose interest and motivation. You are off sick more. You have mounting excuses for poor performance. You burn out.

One of the most positive acts you can do is to identify your weaknesses and accept them. That clears the way for you to manage them. This is not an easy task but it is easier than trying to repair or overcome a weakness, and managing weakness is more productive. This has been recognised in economics, where it has been proven that, by building on relative strengths and trading against relative weaknesses, productivity increases for both parties to the trade.

Strategies for managing weakness

- Trade. If you are a strong teacher but a poor administrator take on extra teaching and release the administration to those with a talent in that area.

- Form strategic alliances. Two or more persons of complementary strengths and weaknesses can be a formidable team, much stronger than the sum of the individuals.

- Find substitutes. If you are not a good public speaker then don't give formal lectures: be creative with other methods of teaching.

7.3 Have a mission

Your strengths can motivate a mission and a mission can motivate your strengths.

The meaning of mission

A personal mission statement is the expression of what you want to be, your purpose in life, your values. A mission provides guidance but does not set goals. Goals are your selected means of becoming what you want to be, of achieving your purposes, and expressing your values. Conceiving and writing out a mission statement adds meaning to what one does and explains why one does it.

The following personal mission statement is given here as an example only; no mission statement should be intended as a missionary tract to convert others.

Mission

I will always remember that two wrongs do not make a right. I will cultivate good principles and act on them without regard to short-term disadvantages. I will be open and honest with all, even those who do not respond in the same way. I will maintain a positive attitude.

I will spare others from insult, injury and undue interference, but I will not ignore difficulties through fear or distaste. I will help subordinates build on strength and only address a weakness when it intrudes on the interests of others.

I will check the facts and the perceptions of others before judging. I will be an active listener. I will act professionally and develop my professional skills. I will learn from my mistakes.

I value reason and truth. I value a cool head in times of crisis.

My professional mission is to identify and promote good academic and educational practices.

The mission statement as an anchor

A personal mission statement becomes a source of guidance not only for important life-directing decisions but for the smaller decisions we need to take in the swirl and emotions of our day-to-day activities.

7.4 Keeping going

It is hard to keep going. We can get into the do-nothing rut and start to believe that we have no control. But we can adopt strategies to help us to keep going.

Be clear and explicit to yourself

You can remind yourself of your mission and goals (long- and medium-term) on a regular basis. This means that you must write them down and have easy access to them. Is your diary a good place? Do you have a personal organiser? What about having some password-protected personal files in your word-processor?

Use visualisation

You can observe yourself as though you were another. If you find changes that are attractive to you, you may be motivated. The clearer and more detailed a picture you have of what you want to be, the more likely you are to allow change. Sports psychologists know the value of athletes' visualising winning performances in order to improve their actual performance. Similarly, by practising visualisation you will help to resolve the difficulties of self-development.

Be informed

Research what you want. It is difficult to get a real picture of what you want unless you become informed about it. You could start by more closely observing and reflecting on things about you. You could read about what you want and talk to appropriate people and ask their advice.

Involve others

We can involve others by telling them about our goals and asking for feedback, support or guidance.

Self-monitor

It has been found that keeping records of any kind can serve as a reinforcement. An early exponent of this technique was Benjamin Franklin, who set himself various self-development tasks and explicitly monitored his performance. For example, he would chart over thirteen weeks the occurrence of new behaviour which he intended to substitute for some former pattern that he deemed unacceptable. Over the period he drove the incidence of unacceptable behaviour down to 0. He would then take another concern and chart that over the next thirteen weeks, and so on. You can chart anything – either something you want to encourage or something you want to discourage. The intention to change, plus the very act of self-monitoring may actually bring about change in your behaviour.

7.5 Traps

Change means going through awkward patches. These are inevitable when you attempt significant change. If you are sympathetic to yourself, you accept your mistakes and feelings of awkwardness.

Discipline

Discipline is not a question of an iron will. It is a matter of avoiding traps when dealing with awkward patches.

Trap: fear of failure

If I try, I'll probably fail. So why try? Fear of failure is at the root of many excuses for not trying. Doubt about one's real worth is the usual cause. The way out of this trap is to dissociate success and failure from one's worth and self-respect. For even success cannot give you a sense of worth: such doubt means that you would not believe in your successes, and success becomes empty.

Accept that success and failure are not the issue, your self-respect is. If you make self-respect the focus of your efforts then you may keep your motivation. You can earn self-respect by trying: the issue is not whether you succeed or fail but whether you commit yourself wholeheartedly to working hard on something you think worthwhile. We all need the experience of pride in facing our fears. We would all like the pleasure of achieving our goals, but we need to know that we can only gain fulfilment through self-respect. Self-respect depends on working hard on something you think worthwhile.

Trap: self-doubt

Self-doubt is usually embedded in our sense of identity and thus influences our whole life. You will not, however, reach your potential as long as you are obsessed with your worth, or rather lack of it. You will be afraid to look and feel awkward. Rather than sifting through the evidence for conclusive proof that your doubts are justified, why not ask yourself a constructive question: 'What is the most meaningful use of my time?' This, of course, is an extremely difficult question to answer, but using this book may help you.

Trap: projection

Projection means being blind to some part of yourself while being very sensitive to that characteristic in others. You hook on to a manifestation of the characteristic in others and project motivations and other negative connotations which are more to do with you than them. As projection is a form of blindness it is an obstacle to your ability to realise your goals. To avoid this trap, think about the quality or qualities that most irritate and annoy you in others. If your reaction to them is tense and emotional, you may be projecting. If you just cannot stand people who get a little angry, ask yourself if it is you who is angry, and so on.

Trap: identification with what has gone

When you feel frustrated and constricted, you are probably looking at things and behaving in ways that have become outdated. If things are changing around you, looking at things as though they were the same, and behaving the same, make you feel increasingly debilitated. The thing to do is to return to identifying strengths and setting long-term goals. Devote your energy to visualising the new and withdraw energy from the old patterns of behaviour.

7.6 Handling put-downs

It may be that some remark saps your confidence or undermines your professional image. These remarks are hard to handle without aggravating the effects. But it can be done, and you should try to defuse the put-down, as it can attack your motivation.

The definition of a put-down

Anything that you feel puts you down is a put-down. You should not worry about whether a put-down was intended as such or not. That is not the point. Remember the golden rule.

The golden rule

The golden rule is: when you feel put-down always respond as if it were a put-down.

Take your time to respond

Take time to think. You need not be quick-witted. Take a moment to think of an effective answer.

Do not explain yourself: get others to explain themselves

Your answer to most people should be a statement of fact or a question of fact. The aim is not to explain yourself but to get others to explain themselves. There are no stock responses which will work for you. You have to work out your own. You will develop your own style and your responses will come more easily and fluently. Remember, though: your only aim is to handle the put-down, not to top it.

- Suppose someone says to you 'You haven't filed the memo on X from Personnel.' Don't answer: 'I didn't even have the memo, I don't get them.' Say instead: 'You are jumping to conclusions. Why do you think I should have received the memo?' With this response, they have to explain themselves.

- Suppose someone says to you: 'I'm getting fed up with all the trouble you are causing.' Don't say: 'I'm not causing trouble, it's the others,' or: 'I'm sorry I can't help it, I'm having a bad patch at the moment.' Say instead: 'How come you are in such a bad mood today?' or: 'Was that a put-down?'

If you want to deepen the communication

There are times when you will want not only to handle the put-down but also deepen the communication. In this case, you might put in your response something more personal.

- Suppose someone says to you: 'You haven't published a good paper in the last year.' Don't answer: 'I tried as hard as I could.' Say instead: 'I feel put down, Fred, because you don't give me credit getting the new grant'.

7.7 Identifying a reference group

What is your reference group?

Your professional reference group are those significant people in your life who you feel you learn from, who are empathetic when you have problems, who feel good when you succeed, and whose approval you like to have. They are not necessarily friends, nor have you necessarily known them well or for a long time. They may never have met all together and may not even know of each other's existence. They are the people you would call together, if you could, in order to help you when you had important decisions to make.

Are the members aware they are members?

Do the members of your professional reference group know they are members? Why not let them know and explain that you are trying to identify and build on potential strengths? Ask them if they would see you every six months and discuss your activities. They will usually be honoured to help.

What is your relationship to each member?

Your relationship to any person is the sum of your responses to each other. What are the characteristics of your relationships with members of your reference group? Compile a list of their names, and beside each name write why that person is a member of your reference group.

Review the list and ask yourself if there are any common reasons. If there are, you have learned something potentially of great value, for relationships help us to define who we are and what our potential is.

What would you have to be like to be in your colleague's reference group?

Do you think you are in your colleague's reference group? What would you have to be like to be a member of their reference group? Learning to be a good colleague could help you to develop professionally and personally. Consider this and ways of behaving which would put you in your colleague's reference group.

One way to earn a place in someone's reference group is to see your colleagues in terms of their strengths.

8 Home and away

Your life is a whole, and therefore to be an organised and effective academic involves addressing every facet of your life. Consider extending the ideas in this book to all facets of your life. In this chapter there are two sections on matters connected with your home life, another on preparing for travel and another on being a foreigner.
The final section is about your participation in societies and conferences.

8.1 Household matters

Here follow a few tips, hints and reminders.

Cleaning

There are firms that specialise in blitz cleaning. If you can afford it, it is efficient to use these firms for specific tasks like spring cleaning. But they also undertake regular maintenance and cleaning tasks; if you give them a schedule they will come in every two weeks and undertake the major tasks, leaving you with only the tidying-up jobs. In the light of your goals, bringing in contractors may not be the extravagance it might at first appear.

Bring things to you

- Find vendors who will deliver, or failing that have a pick-up service.

- Find a hairdresser who will cut your hair at home.

- If you have them, get the kids to earn their pocket money by running errands.

Extended To Dos

To keep track of your household task, make a household book, or extend your organiser to include a household section. You will find that having all household information in one place with your work needs is useful. Keep lists on:

- To Do

- To Call

- To Fix

- To Buy

You can create categories as you need them for your household organiser or section of your personal organiser. Consider the things below.

Emergency list

- The address of the nearest hospital and a map of how to get there.

- Name and address of your physician.

- Name and address of emergency childcare (arrange mutual cover with a friend).

- Medical details of you and your family (everybody's full name, blood type, allergies, if any, and medical histories).

- Emergency repair numbers: gas, electricity, plumbing.

Copy your emergency list and leave it in various places in the house.

Health records

Each member of the family should have a personal record of:

- visits to the doctor;

- the reason for the visit;

- the advice, treatment or medication given.

Make sure that the record shows clearly the nature and date of vaccinations. If you have a recurrent problem that you think might be a mere irritant, chart its occurrences over a period, then check it out with the physician, showing the chart.

Other lists

- Birthdays and other fixed events.
- Checklists for planning travel, parties and so on.
- Repair and maintenance schedules for your house.
- Cleaning schedules.

Planning a gathering

Any gathering requires some planning, but a student gathering needs special attention.

- Set a budget.
- Decide on the type of gathering you are having (bring a bottle, your drinks and nibbles, sit-down, weekend lunch, open house) and make sure the students know exactly what to expect. Avoid students turning up starving to find only drinks and nibbles, or having eaten and finding dinner.
- For some gatherings, it might be appropriate to make your invitations RSVP, and when you have the replies to make up a guest list to circulate, giving a few details of each person.
- File the list.
- Consider purchasing a pile of cheap glasses and white 'party plates' instead of using plastic and paper ones.
- Consider moving furniture or borrowing chairs as needed.
- If you are organising the gathering on your own, select at least some dishes you can cook ahead and freeze.
- Make sure there is provision for vegetarians.
- The only really safe meats in an ethnically mixed group are lamb and chicken.
- If you are providing drinks, work out an average consumption per person. As a rough guide assume that each person will drink:
- one third of a bottle of wine;
- a quarter of a bottle of non-alcoholic wine;
- half a bottle of water or mineral water;
- a quarter of a pint of beer.
- Keep aside a few spare bottles of everything to bring out only if really needed.
- After the gathering, make a note on the guest list of things that could have gone better, comments on the food and drinks, etc.
- Review your lists when planning the next gathering.

8.2 Finance

A general matter that needs special attention is finance.

Files

- Keep all your paperwork and cheque stubs, etc., in a date file (see § 1.4 Filing) and at the end of the year, to be on the safe side, archive the material for the six years (some things you are required to save that long for tax purposes).

- Get a concertina file, or desk file, and make a House file with sections such as Gas, Electricity, Car, etc., and sections for Unpaid Bills and Miscellaneous Receipts. Use this for a year and archive it whole at the end of the year.

- Any expenditure on the house and associated information should be kept in a permanent file and sorted out and handed over to the buyer when you sell your house.

- Compile a personal details list of your bank identification numbers, phone numbers, driving licence, national insurance, credit cards, pension plan policy, insurance numbers and so on. Keep it in a secure place.

Cheque book and bank account

- Make sure you note the details of every transaction in your cheque book.

- Make sure you record all deposits.

- Keep a running balance.

- Reconcile your balance with that on your bank statement.

- Make check marks on cheques and deposits accounted for.

- Draw a circle by those that have not yet appeared on the statement.

- Calculate the adjustments and check that the balances are the same.

Credit cards

- Make sure you record every item of expenditure and payment you make.

- Reconcile your balance with the statement.

- Credit cards are convenient but expensive if used indiscriminately. Keep a running total on the charges to encourage you to see the cost of your transactions.

Paying bills

- Keep all shop receipts for small items in the Miscellaneous Receipts section of your House file. Some of these you will need to cross-check with the bill or credit card statement.

- Retrieve the bills that need paying from the Unpaid Bills section of your system and make out the cheque or fill in the credit card payment section. Give additional identifying information on the cheque, for example, a credit card payment would have your credit card number. On your cheque stub record identifying information, including the reference number and date.

- Mark on your cheque stubs the word 'tax' on any tax-deductible items. (This will help you when filling in your tax returns. For allowable charitable donations make sure you have a confirmation slip.)

- Mark the bill as 'paid', date it and put on the cheque number. File in the appropriate section of your House file.

Budgeting

If you do not know how to use a spreadsheet consider using one to make a budget as an introductory exercise. Spreadsheets usually come with a few simple templates that you can modify to give you ideas and help you to get started.

Income

You will need to determine your regular income by the month and your one-off items (for example, bonus payments, examiners fees, royalties).

Expenditure

You will need to determine your regular expenditure by the month and separately identify your large one-offs and variable items (for example, holiday, savings, entertainment).

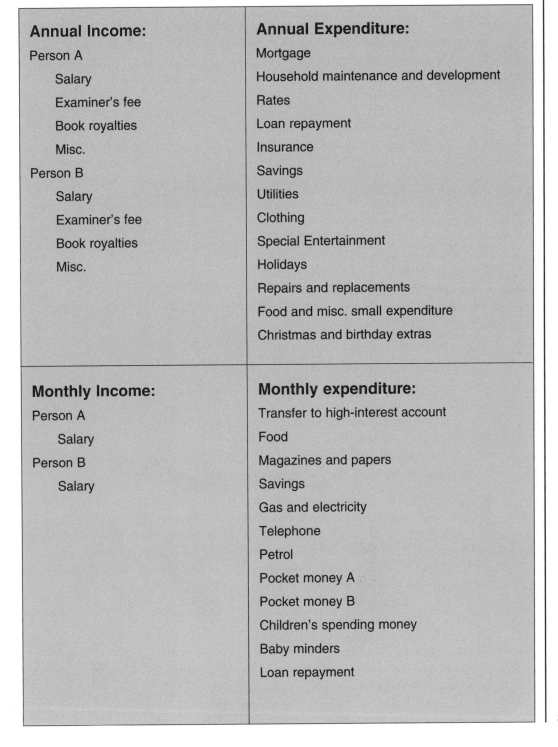

Annual Income:	Annual Expenditure:
Person A	Mortgage
Salary	Household maintenance and development
Examiner's fee	Rates
Book royalties	Loan repayment
Misc.	Insurance
Person B	Savings
Salary	Utilities
Examiner's fee	Clothing
Book royalties	Special Entertainment
Misc.	Holidays
	Repairs and replacements
	Food and misc. small expenditure
	Christmas and birthday extras
Monthly Income:	**Monthly expenditure:**
Person A	Transfer to high-interest account
Salary	Food
Person B	Magazines and papers
Salary	Savings
	Gas and electricity
	Telephone
	Petrol
	Pocket money A
	Pocket money B
	Children's spending money
	Baby minders
	Loan repayment

Many of your goals need financial provision. Make sure your budget recognises this.

You should consider maintaining three bank accounts: a savings account, a high-interest account (HIA) and a current account. Pay your regular income into your current account. Pay your irregular income into your HIA. Each month you need to transfer to your HIA sufficient to pay for the large one-off expenses and variable amounts. For example, if you plan to spend £120 on a holiday you need to transfer £12; if you budget to spend £120 on clothing you will need to transfer another £12. Then, when you pay for holiday items or clothing you take the money from the HIA account (transfer the amount to cash or your credit card as appropriate). You should budget so that at the end of the year you have a surplus as a fallback; convert your actual surplus to savings at the year end. You can keep track of actuals on a monthly basis.

Being an Effective Academic

8.3 Travelling

Travel planning

- Compile a checklist of things to pack.

- Compile a checklist of things to do as you leave (e.g. unplug the TV).

- Compile a list of things you will need to keep with you: directions, itinerary, tickets, passport (has it got the right visa?), foreign currency.

- Have spare passport photographs and a photocopy of your passport to take with you. If your original passport goes missing, the nearest embassy can use the photocopy to issue a new one.

- Ensure that you have all the appropriate directions and flight details.

- Compile an itinerary, including addresses and telephone numbers of places you will be staying; make four copies, one to leave with someone looking after your home, one to give to someone at work, one to put with your documents, one to put in your suitcase so that you can be traced if it gets lost in transit.

Luggage

- Travel light. Most people take far too much luggage with them. With only hand luggage you not only lessen the chances of losing your possessions, you lessen the stress of the journey and can take an hour off its length.

- If your must take a suitcase, keep your lecture notes and presentation material with you as hand luggage (if you lose underwear and toothbrushes, etc., you can buy them when you get there).

- Instead of lugging masses of conference papers and proceedings back with you, sort the papers out, throw away what you don't really need and post home the remainder.

Taxis

Avoid airport taxi touts at all costs. Most airports display warning notices which ask you to use the official taxis. It is simple foolishness to ignore the warnings and to believe anything a tout tells you. If you do get caught, the police will not help and the best you can probably do is haggle the price down a little.

Your room

- When you are first shown your hotel room, check out your bathroom, bed and equipment.

- Get into the habit of looking around; check for the fire exit.

- Thieves steal to sell and usually work quickly; they are not interested in your professional papers, separate them out and lay them openly on a convenient surface.

- Place valuable things and documents in the hotel safe.

- Lock your door and use the spy-hole to see who is knocking.

8.4 When you are abroad you are the foreigner

If you have prepared your visit to a foreign country, you will know something of the country and its manners and customs. And, even though the academic community has a certain internationalism, it is wise to take note of and act upon local custom.

Respect cultural diversity

Japan

The Japanese exchange business cards and expect you to look at them (even if they are in Japanese). You should take plenty of your own with you and exchange cards with everyone at any meeting. It is a good idea to have lots of neatly wrapped token gifts too. Everything is regulated by a strict routine of courtesy. You cannot overestimate the need for mutual respect, friendliness and rapport. If you are in a hurry, or do not indulge in the polite exchanges of conversation and gifts you will be seen as quite rude. This personal dimension is so important that it is very difficult for the Japanese to say 'no'; if you ask the wrong question, prevarication or saying 'yes' are the only polite responses available. For example if you ask them whether they have understood what you have said many will reply 'yes', even if you were totally incomprehensible (to say otherwise might imply that you were at fault in not making yourself clear, and it would be disrespectful to point that out to you).

Arab peoples

Arabs have an ancient tradition of hospitality and politeness.Your Arab host may feel a need to extend hospitality to you even though others are not permitted to eat and drink as it is Ramadan. Acknowledge that it is Ramadan; accept their kindness, but eat and drink with consideration.

The ancient laws of hospitality also mean that there is an inclination to allow interruptions by visitors who will be invited to drink tea and talk. You must accept this and show no signs of impatience. You will find also a reluctance to say 'no'. If you do not properly formulate your questions or propositions, rather than giving a straight 'no', it is likely that your host will evade the issue and play for time in order give room for manoeuvre or for the matter be forgotten. In business dealings it is best to treat all concerned as parties to a consultation, using locutions like 'I was thinking about suggesting that . . .What do you think?'

The USA

In the USA things move faster, and to be seen to be in a hurry is no bad thing. In fact, having too little to do is a sign of failure. Because of the pace, things go wrong, and complaining and handling grievances are widespread skills. Being assertive is equated with rapid loud talking. If you take the style too seriously and personally and think it an indication of Americans' morality you will be making a mistake. The people are as warm and generous as any other and are just as likely to establish enduring relationships.

The US citizen experiences a high standard of living and believes that anybody has the opportunity to reach even higher standards by self-improvement through hard work. This can be summarised as follows. The US has social stratification (like every society) but not a class system (like Britain). They have very little envy and have a 'good on you' attitude if you do well. They are entirely professional in their approach and professionalism is the only thing that is likely to engage and impress them.

Respect individual diversity

There will be many Japanese academics who are more American than many from the USA and there will be American academics who are Bedouin in disguise. It is derogatory to ignore the potentially wide range of individual diversity on the basis of national or racial characteristics.

84

8.5 Societies and conferences

Most academics attend society meetings and conferences, occasionally to give a paper. This section tries to help you to use these activities to promote your interests.

Societies

*   Join only a few societies and participate fully; don't neglect the smaller local societies.

*   Present good papers; don't be persuaded that pot boilers are acceptable.

*   At meetings, always introduce yourself with your name and affiliation.

*   Talk to people about their research, not yours. You may talk about your research, after a request, but don't make the mistake of taking the request too seriously.

*   If you can join the committee, execute any task exceptionally well. Never take half measures. If you get elected to an important position cultivate your predecessor who will usually help informally.

*   Carefully study major figures. They can be an important source of learning. They are usually multi-skilled, as well as superb at their craft.

Attending a conference

What is a conference? You might answer this question best by seeing what going to a conference makes possible. A conference enables personal interaction with friends, peers and authorities. You will remember good conferences for precisely these categories of interaction and the setting in which the interactions took place. The foundation of a conference is the sessions and papers, but they are not the total. A conference is quite properly a mixture of social and intellectual stimulation.

*   Plan to attend only those parts of relevance to you.

*   Read the abstract in the conference proceedings and plan out which papers you should go to.

*   Do not sit through a whole session on the basis of some misguided notion that this is what you are supposed to do. There is no stigma attached to you or the next speaker if, at the end of the paper you wanted to hear, you quietly go.

*   When you go to listen to a speaker, do not merely sit there. On analogy with active reading, consider what questions the paper and presentation should be answering for you. You might want to prepare these explicitly when deciding on which sessions to attend.

You should have some commitment to the society hosting the meeting or the conference, and you should consider as part of your commitment attendance at its special events.Plan to attend:

*   all keynote speeches;

*   invited lectures;

*   panel sessions;

*   other special events in areas of interest.

As well as being the best way of supporting the conference, these are usually the most effective way to get a good overview and find out what are the real issues.

The rest of the time plan to spend with friends, peers and authorities.

*   The luncheons and banquets are a waste of time unless you ensure that you get a table with people you want to meet.

*   The gatherings for cocktails are the best bet and you should always go to these. Get there on time and have serious discussions early. Leave with friends when the place gets packed.

85

Remember that some of your colleagues have spent a great deal of time organising the meeting. No public display of irritation with equipment and facilities is warranted. Work round the difficulties. Learn a lesson and make sure you don't make the same mistake when you run a conference. If, on the other hand, the difficulties are the result of shortcomings on the part of a paid organising company, then it is desirable to seek immediate remedy and if this is not possible to write afterwards to the chair of the conference and suggest improvements.

Presentation of a paper

At some time or other you will have to present a paper. To be effective you cannot neglect preparation and present it badly. The following are some guidelines.

- Do not leave the preparation too late and take photocopies of typed tables or notes. On no account rough draw a few slides in the hotel the night before. Your slides must be readable: six words per line and six lines per slide are a good rule of thumb. Use colour on no more than 60% of your slides and do not use more than three colours.

- Run through and practise the presentation in advance and make sure you can deliver it in time.

- The introduction should be as good as you can make it. The body of the talk should emphasise results and interpretations, rather than techniques. Involve the audience. Take, if only for a moment, a look around the room. Relax, smile.

- Never apologise for any shortcomings you think you perceive in your presentation. If something outside of your control goes wrong and intrudes, try to be calm and see the humour in it. Your best bet is to assume that something will go wrong and plan your response. Relax, smile.

- Do not read every word. Neither should your talk be a slide presentation. Slides must be an adjunct to what you say. If the slide projector fails do not try to put it right and don't let anyone else attempt to do so. Do not comment. Use your slides as hand cards and calmly carry on. Relax, smile.

- Engage the audience, look at people's faces, even if only for a moment. Speak as though you care. Be especially careful if you are in a dead period (first session after lunch). Make sure you have some trick up your sleeve to grab their attention. This might be nothing more than a very powerful image and good modulation of your voice. You cannot make a professional presentation in the dark, so do not permit the organisers to plunge the room into darkness; subdued lighting is the most you should tolerate.

- Present conclusions in a way that invites comments and discussion. If you are prepared properly and there is time for discussion, do not treat every question and comment as an attack and respond accordingly. If you feel nervous try active listening. Keep asking questions until it is clear that it is not an attack or until the chair moves the discussion on. Relax, smile.

- Do not run over time: your audience will not listen anyway – they will be busy being embarrassed for you, and wondering when you are going to stop.

Effective presentation of papers depends on a conscious learning process. Consider making it one of your goals to be good at presenting your ideas. Knowledge is necessarily shared and it is your duty to enable the audience to participate in the adventure.

Do not lose sight of the fact that meetings should be enjoyable.